DR. CHARLES M. LEE

ENCOURAGEMENT FOR SUCH A TIME AS THIS

40 HEARTWARMING STORIES TO **LIFT** **YOUR** **SPIRITS**

Printed in the United States of America.

Cover Design by 100Covers.com
Interior Design by FormattedBooks.com

A NOTE FROM THE AUTHOR

Writing a book is more than putting thoughts on paper. It's a process of building bridges that will connect author and reader.

The teacher in me wants to extend the bridges of communication beyond the book's ending. I want to keep the conversation going and encourage the reader to explore the topics further.

To do this, I created a Reader's Study/Discussion Guide that can be used while reading the book, or after completing it. It can be used by one person for personal study or by two or more people to stimulate dialogue.

If you would like a Guide, please follow the steps outlined above. And may the bridges be both thought-provoking and encouraging.

For Muriel,
who has been my wife, friend,
and faithful encourager for over 60 years,
and for my children,
grandchildren and great-grandchildren.
They all light up my life
and lift my spirits.

The Book of Esther tells a beautiful story of
ENCOURAGEMENT.
Times were difficult.
An entire race of people was about to perish.
Esther, a woman of strength, wisdom, and courage
became Queen
"for such a time as this"
and saved her people.
(Esther 4:14)

No matter how difficult life can be
or what fears you may have,
BE ENCOURAGED.
God is present
"for such a time as this.

CONTENTS

INTRODUCTION

There's a time for everything, and a season
for every activity under heaven.
—Ecclesiastes 3·1

This is a book about encouragement.

"For such a time as this," when people are faced with fear and conflict in the world, they need to be reassured that things are going to be okay. They need to feel secure and hopeful about the future.

That's what you will find in this book: words of encouragement that will inspire you to be strong in the face of life's struggles and challenges. You will discover positive ways to deal with difficult times. And you will read stories and anecdotes about how to live a happy, fulfilled life.

Thomas Paine's famous statement, "These are the times that try men's souls," seems as appropriate today as it did in 1776 when he penned *Common Sense*. His goal was to encourage people to unite and not give up hope. And it worked. His powerful words of encouragement helped to recharge the revolutionary cause that led to independence.

Like Thomas Paine, I believe the human spirit is strong. It can survive almost anything. History has proven this to be true. But even when people are strong and stand tall in the face of fear and uncertainty, they still need encouragement. And often all it takes is a few words, aptly spoken, to inspire them.

As a former college professor and mental health counselor, I've spent over 50 years teaching and counseling with people of all ages. I've listened carefully to what they had to say — their struggles, their hopes, their fears, their dreams, as well as their fun, creative experiences. What they shared with me over the years gave me insights into two things that seemed to benefit them the most: words of encouragement, aptly spoken, and a caring attitude. These are the same benefits that are offered in this book.

I didn't start out to write a book. In my retirement, I simply enjoyed having the time to write anecdotes and stories that were encouraging in nature. After I had accumulated quite a few of these, I began sharing some of them with family and friends. The feedback was positive. In fact, many suggested that I put the writings in a book format so others could enjoy them as well. After thinking about it for a while, I decided I would give it a try. Sometimes that's what a person has to do. Stop thinking about it and just do it.

It was difficult to choose which writings should go in this book, but I finally settled on 40 that I thought would work best. The writings are brief and in no particular order. You can pick and choose what you want to read. Each one touches on one or more of 9 different themes. At the end of each story are three positive statements to stimulate further reflection.

The 9 themes represent what might be considered a basic philosophy of life — exploring such questions as, "Who am I?" "What is my purpose?" and "Where am I going?" I've used these themes to be helpful and encouraging to the people I've worked with over the years. Here's a brief description of the 9 themes:

- Laugh often — laughter is medicine that makes you feel better.
- Learn from nature, the world's greatest classroom — it teaches all you need know about how to live life, maintain balance, and survive.
- Do the things that make you feel young at heart — have fun, imagine, explore, play, sing, dance, jump rope, go to the circus, eat cotton candy.
- Share your love and treat others the way you want to be treated.
- Focus on things that really matter in life — let go of the rest.
- Strengthen the bridges in your relationships — build new ones if necessary.
- Believe in the creative spirit that's within you and give yourself permission to express it.
- Feed on things that nourish you spiritually, mentally, and physically.
- Dream big, set goals, and persevere.

DR. CHARLES M. LEE

Perhaps more than anything else, I've learned that life doesn't have to be complicated. The simpler it is the better. It all boils down to two basic things that people want in life:

- They want to be happy.
- They want to feel vibrant, healthy and safe.

I can't personally think of two more meaningful goals. After all, who doesn't want to be happy? And who doesn't want to wake up each morning and feel full of life? Who doesn't want to wake up with a positive outlook on life and look forward to the blessings of the day?

These are the things I write about in this book. Heartwarming things that are positive and encouraging. Things that will lift your spirits and give you hope.

I invite you to come with me, take a journey through the book, and be encouraged.

Grab a cup of coffee or tea and find a cozy chair. Let's enjoy some time together.

A CREATIVE SPIRIT DWELLS WITHIN YOU

Creativity is simply allowing the child within you to speak.

Let me say a few words about creativity before we get into the rest of the book. Creativity plays a vital role in how we view life and how we experience it. It's a major factor in our ability to enjoy life and be happy. Research has shown that it affects our health and well-being. It contributes to the longevity of life.

Unfortunately most adults make little use of the creativity that's within them and thus miss out on its many benefits. They know there's something missing in their life but can't figure out what it is. They just know they feel unfulfilled. Hopefully, as we journey through this book together, we will see how important creativity is to adults and how easy it is to express it in everyday life.

I love the memories I have of childhood that involved imagination and creative thinking. The whole world of my friends and me was an imaginary stage. We played our version of the roles we had come to love from watching movies and television.

One day I was Tarzan in the deep, dark jungle. (My little brother didn't enjoy having to play the role of Cheetah, the monkey, but he usually agreed to do it.) We made spears out of tall weeds and a hut out of bales of straw. I lost track of how many times we saved Jane from being kidnapped by savages. She always trusted that we would get there in time. And we did.

On another day I was Roy Rogers, riding my faithful horse, Trigger. My horse was an old broom that had been tossed out of the kitchen. How proud my friends and I were to save the town from the outlaws who wanted to rob our bank. In our world of fantasy, good always triumphed over evil.

And how can I forget the many summer evenings my cousins and I performed intricate surgery on fireflies. We set up a hospital by draping old sheets over the clothes line and used a pocket knife as our scalpel. We were perhaps the first doctors to experiment with transplants. In our minds, we saved the lives of hundreds of fireflies.

Oh the joy of childhood when imagination and fantasy are alive and vivid and know no bounds. Every child knows how to think creatively, to think outside the box, to invent, to experiment, to innovate. Every child is a creator and knows how to see something that doesn't exist and bring it into being. What a powerful gift. I'm convinced that childhood creativity is a spiritual experience because it involves belief, faith, trust and creation.

But what happens when we become adults? What causes us to stop creating? What causes us to even deny that we have any creativeness within us? In working with adults for many years I've heard the majority of them say, "I don't have an ounce of creativity in me. I wish I did, but I don't."

The fact is, however, each one of us is blessed with the spirit of creativity, whether we recognize it or not, and whether we agree or not. Trust me, there's a wonderful creative spirit that dwells in each of us. Isn't it interesting how we can easily see it in a child's imaginative play, or an artist's paintings, or a concert pianist's performance, or an inventor's invention, but we can't see it in ourselves. Isn't it interesting that we know we had it as a child, but we don't believe we have it as an adult.

I happen to admire the cutting-edge research on creativity in adults by Dr. Gene Cohen of George Washington University. He was a psychiatrist, geriatrician (a specialist in the health concerns of aging), a scientist, and a public policy activist on behalf of older Americans. In my opinion, his outstanding body of work stands as one of the greatest contributions ever made to the field of gerontology.

Cohen believed that creativity is innate. No matter how you define it, no matter what your gender, race, ethnicity, or spiritual view is, creativity is a basic human attribute. Everyone has it.

He believed that we are blind to the powerful effect creativity can have on our lives. Even when we recognize the value of creativity, we often remain blind to the presence of creativity in our own lives.

Part of the problem is that our understanding of creativity is clouded by stereotypes, negative myths, misunderstandings, prejudice and ignorance. It's further clouded by believing that creativity belongs only to the few, such as the artist, the musician, or the author.

Cohen explored the powerful potential that creativity brings to individuals. His research made it clear that adults who engage in some form of ongoing creative activities will experience important benefits. The benefits are immediate and long-lasting. Two of these key benefits are listed here. Read them carefully and believe.

1. Creative experiences help you become more resilient and better able to cope with life's adversities and losses.
2. Creativity contributes to physical health. Creative expression boosts the immune system and fosters feelings that improve one's outlook and a sense of well-being.

Cohen's research confirms what I have personally viewed in adults as I worked with them over the years. Creativity can indeed be stimulated in every person. I have seen it unfold in individuals from all walks of life, and in all age groups, including older adults in their 80s and 90s.

Creativity can come alive in us just like it did in childhood. We can imagine, dream, discover, think outside the box, and create. And when we do, Cohen says we will be happier, healthier, and see life in a more positive light.

Let me say it again. A creative spirit dwells within you. Forget the myths you've heard about creativity and all the traditional definitions. Think of creativity in its broadest sense.

So much of what creativity is deals with problem-solving. If you want to make soup but don't have all the ingredients, you modify it and create your own recipe. That's creativity. If your child's toy breaks and you don't have the exact parts to fix it, you think of a way to fix it your own way. That's creativity. If you do a crossword puzzle, or put together a picture puzzle, that's a creative experience. If you watch a movie or attend a concert, that's a creative experience.

So keep doing creative things. Keep the creative experience within you alive. Believe that you are creative because you are. And here's good news. The more creatively involved you are, the more encouraged you will be. There's a direct link between the two. When you create, you accomplish. When you accomplish something, you feel encouraged.

Much of what is in this book shows how easily creativity can be expressed, regardless of age or circumstances. It's within you. All you have to do is believe it's there and express it.

REFLECTION

1. Creative minds do common things in an uncommon way.
2. Those who create are those who believe they can.
3. *He has gifted them with the know-how for carving, designing, weaving, and embroidering in blue, purple, and scarlet fabrics, and in fine linen. They can make anything and design anything.* —Exodus 35:35

SOMETIMES YOU HAVE TO LAUGH AT YOURSELF

A joyful heart is good medicine
—Proverbs 17:22

It was 1949. The League of Nations became the United Nations. Elvis Presley received his first guitar. The movie *It's a Wonderful Life* premiered. Jackie Robinson became the first African American to play for a Minor League baseball team. And I became a proud third grade angel.

I knew I was an angel because I heard it chanted by classmates as they jumped rope at recess: "First grade babies, second grade tots, *third grade angels*, fourth grade snots." It was a tradition that third graders were little angels.

The truth is, though, I was no angel. I often did things to make classmates laugh. I had the ability to distort my face to look like a monkey or a hyena or some other goofy character. But the face that got the most laughs was my imitation of Mrs. Young, our teacher. I could purse my lips, wrinkle my eyebrows, and give a stern glare just like she did.

It was common knowledge that Mrs. Young rarely smiled and never laughed out loud. Whenever there was a classroom disruption, she would clap her hands and say, "Remember, children, we're here to learn, not to laugh."

I confess that I enjoyed making my classmates laugh when they weren't supposed to be laughing. For instance, I could easily get a little girl named Judy to squeal with laughter in the middle of a math test. Or I could get Norman to blurt out a loud guffaw when the whole class was supposed to be doing silent reading. I knew what to do to get a good laugh.

Fortunately, Mrs. Young never caught me making faces, but I was certain she knew I was doing something. She would often glare at me after someone's laughter had disrupted the class. Her icy stare was enough to make me settle down, at least for a while.

One day in early November I was at recess and thought of a funny antic to perform. I jumped in one of the swings and pumped as high as I could go. I yelled for my classmates to look at me.

I wrinkled my nose, squinted my eyes, and formed a harsh look on my face. "Look, everyone, I'm Mrs. Young," I said, "Now don't you dare laugh. Remember, children, we're here to learn, not to laugh."

As I was doing my impression and getting some good laughs, the bell rang. Everyone ran to get in line. In a rush, I leaped from the swing and felt my jeans somehow catch on the chain. I heard a ripping sound. Once I landed on my feet, I felt the back of my jeans and discovered that my pocket was ripped half off. There was a large hole that exposed my long johns. My mother had made me put on long johns because of the chilly weather.

I panicked. With my long johns exposed, I feared I would be the laughing stock of the whole school. I enjoyed making others laugh but I certainly didn't like the idea of being laughed at.

I decided I would use one of the other doors to the school. My plan was to run to the classroom and get in my seat before the other children arrived. When I got to the classroom, Mrs. Young was at her desk. She asked me what I was doing. I explained that I had torn my jeans and didn't want the other children to see the big hole in the rear of my pants. I was too embarrassed to say the words "long johns."

Mrs. Young stared at me for a moment, perhaps debating in her mind whether this was one of my silly antics. Finally she asked if I would like for her to sew the hole shut. I almost hugged her but knew better. I simply shook my head affirmatively.

Mrs. Young told me to go to the cloakroom and stay out of sight until she came and got me. The cloakroom was a room behind the teacher's desk where my classmates would not be able to see me.

My classmates entered the classroom and went to their seats. Mrs. Young told them to put their head down and rest and not look up until she gave them the signal. She then came to the cloakroom and got me.

She whispered for me to crawl on top of her desk and lie on my stomach. I was hesitant to do so but did as she said. She reached in her desk drawer, pulled out a needle and thread, and proceeded to sew the tear in my pants. As she was finishing, her hand evidently slipped and the needle dug into my skin. I let out a screech that startled the children. They looked up and saw me sprawled across Mrs. Young's desk. They knew they shouldn't laugh, but they did.

I felt humiliated. I jumped off the desk and wanted to run out of the room. I shook my fist at my classmates as though to warn them not to laugh, but that just made them laugh all the more. I looked at Mrs. Young and got a humongous shock. Even she had a smile on her face. I got another shock when she put her hand over her mouth and laughed out loud. At that point, I had to laugh as well.

From that day forward I stopped trying to be funny at other people's expense. The jab from Mrs. Young's needle made me realize that it wasn't fun to be laughed at.

What the children didn't know and what Mrs. Young didn't know was what I discovered when I got home. Mrs. Young had sewn my jeans to my long johns. That made me have another good laugh about the whole event.

I couldn't help but wonder though if Mrs. Young's jab with the needle was an accident or intentional. Either way it was a lesson learned.

I must admit that I felt a sense of satisfaction about the whole incident. After all, I not only got the whole class to laugh, but got Mrs. Young to laugh as well — out loud.

We all know what a good laugh does to our overall mood. It has the power to heal both body and soul. It's like medicine that makes us feel better. It's like experiencing free therapy. It lifts our spirits.

George Bernard Shaw once said, "You don't stop laughing when you grow old, you grow old when you stop laughing." There's a lot of truth in that quote. So, to feel young and vibrant, keep laughing, even if you have to laugh at yourself.

REFLECTION

1. Laughter adds life to your years and puts wrinkles in all the right places.
2. One of the quickest ways to grow old is to stop laughing.
3. *A happy heart makes the face cheerful.* —Proverbs 15:13

THE GREASED PIG CAPER

It's okay to love a pig.

When I was a teenager I used to spend a few weeks each summer with my cousin, Bill. He lived in Bowling Green, Ohio. His home was just a few blocks from the city park where the Wood County Fair was held.

On one of my visits with Bill, we decided to be adventurous and go to the fair. We didn't have much money to spend on rides and side shows, but we thought it would be fun to just enjoy the sights and sounds of a small town fair.

As a kid who lived on a farm, going to the fair was a special treat. I soaked it in. Hot dogs and popcorn never smelled so good. I was intrigued by such things as the 600 pound lady who had a foot long beard, the Tazmanian devil who had to be kept in a cage, the strong man who could hold the rubber sledge hammer in one hand and ring the bell at the High Striker attraction, the lady who was half woman and half reptile, and the haunted house where supposedly some people entered but never came out.

Oh, the fun and nostalgia of a small town fair. Every kid should experience it. There's something about it that brings out the child in us and creates memories that last a lifetime.

Speaking of memories, here's one I'll never forget. Bill and I were strolling through the fair grounds when we noticed a sign that said, "Greased Pig Contest." A man standing beside the sign urged us to get in line and try to catch a greased pig. We had never heard of a greased pig contest, but the man said it was free so we decided to give it a try.

While we were in line, we could hear kids yelling, pigs squealing, and the crowd roaring with laughter. We wondered what it was all about. We soon found out.

When we got near the arena gate where the event was taking place, a man said to us, "Listen up. There are greased pigs in here. You'll have 5 minutes to try and catch one. Now, count off. Only 8 can go in at a time."

We counted off and I was number 4. I don't know why, but I always considered 4 to be my lucky number. I was sure I would catch a pig.

The man opened the gate and 8 of us entered. My group included 6 boys and 2 girls. In the arena were several heavily greased pigs. I don't recall how many.

Someone blew a whistle, the pigs began to run and squeal, and the crowd began to roar. Bill and I glanced at each other, then headed for the pigs. I leaped for one only to have it slip through my hands and leave me coated with grease. This happened several more times and I got greasier and greasier. At one point I looked at Bill and, with a face heavily coated with grease, he gave me a look that said, "Why are we doing this?"

Some man yelled, "One minute left," and I still had no pig. I was determined to get one. A small greased pig, being chased by a heavily greased boy, came running past me. I thought, "This is my last chance." I launched forward, landed on the pig, wrapped my greased arms around it, and held on. It squealed, wiggled and wriggled, but I somehow held on. The whistle blew and I had my greased pig.

Bill did not catch a pig but he went with me as we were herded into a tent where several other greased kids were holding their greased pig. Bill whispered to me, "Just look at us. We're covered with grease. My mom's going to kills us." I whispered back, "Maybe she won't recognize us. I can hardly see your face."

A man came in and said, "We will put a tag on your pig with your name on it and place it in the pen behind you. You will have until 5:00 p.m. to pick it up. You are to take it home, feed it, and take care of it for one year. You'll then bring it back for the auction. You'll be allowed to keep the money that is auctioned for your pig."

I was a bit stunned. I had no idea I was supposed to keep the pig. I thought I was simply supposed to catch a pig and maybe get some kind of a prize. I didn't realize the pig was the prize.

Fortunately my dad worked for the State Department of Highways in Bowling Green. I got in touch with him. He was surprised (shocked?) by what I had done. He said he would pick me up after work and take me to get the pig.

My dad and I got the pig and headed home. He told me I could have a pen in the barn for the pig, but it would be my responsibility to take care of it. It made me feel better to know the pig had a place to stay.

I named the pig "Miss Daisy." I have no clue how I came up with that name but it seemed to fit. She was an intelligent pig. Even my grandpa said so. She would follow me around the barnyard and always seemed happy to see me. I guess that's the things about pets. They have a way of making you feel special. If you treat them right, they will like you unconditionally. I wish humans were more like that.

Miss Daisy and I became good friends. She ate well and grew fast. I bought a special brush and kept her groomed. I was faithful about cleaning her pen. I only had one problem with her. The barnyard outside her pen often had puddles in it, especially after a rain. Miss Daisy loved to wallow in those puddles. Sometimes she would do it immediately after I groomed her.

I would bawl Miss Daisy out for wallowing in the mud until I did a little research on why pigs wallow. I discovered that pigs lack functional sweat glands and are basically incapable of panting. To thermo regulate, they rely on wallowing in water or mud to cool the body. The mud provides a cooling layer on the body. This process lowers the pig's temperature by 3.6 degrees Fahrenheit. After I learned this, I let Miss Daisy wallow all she wanted. Besides making her cool, I figured it would be good for her complexion.

The year went fast and soon the fateful day arrived. I had become quite attached to Miss Daisy as a pet. She wasn't just a barnyard animal to me. Before we loaded her on the trailer, I groomed her one last time. I wanted her to look her best. Her face looked almost human as she looked up at me. She batted her long pig eyelashes at me and made me sick about having to part with her. I think somehow she knew what was going to happen.

At the stockyard, those of us who had caught the pigs were required to go into the arena one at a time with our pig. Buyers would study the pigs and make a bid. I watched the owners and the pigs go into the arena ahead of me. The pigs ran wild. The owners had no control over them. It was obvious that the owners and their pigs had not developed a relationship. Raising their pig was just a project. Nothing more.

Things were different when Miss Daisy and I walked into the arena. She weighed in at a solid 275 pounds, was beautifully groomed and well-mannered. Everywhere I walked in the arena to show her off, she followed me. It was like she wanted to look good for me, even though it would be our last moments together.

The audience grew quiet as they watched the remarkable Miss Daisy strut with her head held high. She won them over. Even the auctioneer commented about her appearance and manners as he started the bidding. It was a bidding war but the Kroger Company ended with the high bid. Miss Daisy brought a good price and took all honors. She was named "the most outstanding pig."

After the bidding, I walked her to the gate where the men from the Kroger Company were waiting to take her away. Miss Daisy turned and looked at me. I'll never forget her look. I fell to my knees and gave her a hug. Tears welled in my eyes and rolled down my cheeks. I didn't care who noticed. I gave myself permission to cry right there in front of everyone.

I told Miss Daisy, "You're not just a pig, you're a friend. And I'll always remember you."

And I have remembered her. Every time I see the Kroger name, I think of my Miss Daisy. She gave me one full year of an unforgettable friendship and memories that I still fondly recall.

I never thought about it before the year I spent with Miss Daisy, but the experience made me realize that a pet, even a former greased pig, can be a good friend. She was always glad to see me. She liked me for who I was. She made me feel special. She listened and grunted when I told her how my day went at school. She lifted my spirits. In a way, she did the things that a good friend does. She taught me how to be a friend.

REFLECTION

1. A good friend comes into your life and makes such an impact on your life that you can't remember what life was like without them.
2. You can learn a lot from pets, including pigs. They're masters at unconditional love.
   Love is not a temporary feeling. Feelings change, but unconditional love is everlasting.
3. *A friend loves at all times.*— Proverbs 17:17

THE CLOTHES DON'T MATTER

What's in your heart is what really counts.

I don't know why I chose a cold, snowy day in December to be baptized. It was one week before Christmas in 1955 and, as a high school senior, I was starting to seriously think about what I was going to do with my life.

I lived on a farm and attended a small church in Jerry City, Ohio, a sleepy little town of maybe two hundred people. The church was a small, narrow building, seating maybe seventy people, with a baptistery at the front and two tiny adjacent rooms.

After the pastor's sermon, as the congregation was singing "Just as I Am," I walked down the aisle and told the pastor I wanted to be baptized. The pastor said the water in the baptistery was ice cold and would have to be heated in the afternoon. He asked me to return for the Sunday evening service to be baptized. I normally didn't attend the Sunday evening service but agreed to return for the baptism. I'm not sure why but I didn't tell my parents about my intentions to be baptized, so they were not in attendance.

At the evening service, after the pastor's sermon, I again walked down the aisle to be baptized. One of the deacons took me into one of the tiny rooms adjacent to the baptistery and told me to put on the clothes I had brought for the baptism.

"I didn't know I was supposed to bring clothes," I said.

The congregation was small and baptisms were infrequent. I had never personally witnessed one so I had no clue about the clothes. I had assumed that the church provided some type of baptismal robe.

"Well, you can't be baptized in the clothes you have on," the deacon said. "You'll be wet and freeze to death on the way home. The temperature out there is well below freezing. You'll have to go out the back door and ask one of the neighbors if you can borrow some clothes for the baptism."

I was a shy farm boy and the very thought of going to some stranger's door and asking to borrow clothes for my baptism made me weak in my knees.

"I just don't know if I can do that," I said.

The deacon put his hand on my shoulder and said, "Son, how badly do you want to be baptized?"

That was a good question. With no clothes for the baptism and the wind howling outside the door, I debated in my mind what I should do. Finally I said, "Well, I guess I do."

"Well, then, go find some clothes," the deacon said. "I'll have the congregation sing Christmas carols till you get back. But hurry."

Reluctantly I went out the back door where cold, blowing snow greeted me. I peered down the street to see which houses had lights on and hopefully would have some kind soul inside willing to let me borrow some clothes. Some of the houses had their Christmas lights turned on and I decided to go to the house that looked the brightest and friendliest.

The house I chose was three doors down from the church. I went to the front door, said a brief prayer, took a deep breath, and knocked. A tall, matronly lady answered. I glanced at her dress and apron and immediately thought, *Well, her clothes sure won't work.*

"Excuse me, ma'am," I said, "but I'm from the church down the street and I want to be baptized, The problem is I need to borrow some clothes to wear for the baptism. Do you have any clothes in the house I could borrow? I would really appreciate it and I promise to bring them back."

"Doesn't the church have baptismal robes for that?" she asked.

"No, ma'am, they don't," I said.

"Well, step inside and get out of the cold wind," she said. "We'll see what we can do."

I was relieved to be invited in and was greeted by the woman's husband. He was a tall, burly man about twice my size and wearing bib overalls. I looked at the large overalls and thought, *No way will his clothes work either.*

After a brief conversation, the wife said they had an adult daughter that lived with them and suggested that maybe she had something I could wear. My heart sank. *A lady's clothes?* I wanted to run out the door and go find another house, but I knew it would not be a polite thing to do. The lady told me to sit down while she looked for some clothes. As I sat there, I kept thinking of the congregation at the church singing one Christmas carol after another and wondering what was taking so long for me to change clothes in that little room adjacent to the baptistery.

The woman soon came back with a lady's long sleeved shirt and jeans that zipped up the side. Except for some lace on the shirt's collar, the clothes looked workable...that is, if they fit. I figured I could turn the collar under and hide the lace. As a shy farm boy, I definitely didn't relish the idea of being seen wearing a shirt with lace on it.

After expressing gratitude for the clothes, I headed back through the snow toward the church. As I neared the church, I could see the warm glow of lights coming from the windows. I could hear the congregation singing "Silent Night" as they patiently waited to witness a new birth. A bit of nostalgia grabbed hold of me. I thought of the birth of that baby boy centuries ago, lying in the manger, wrapped in humble strips of cloth, no fancy baby clothes. The clothes didn't matter at all. What mattered was the birth itself.

I went into the little room adjacent to the church baptistery and put on the lady's clothes that were so graciously given to me. They were snug but acceptable. I turned the lace collar under and was ready to be born again. The clothes didn't matter at all. What really mattered was the birth.

"Joy to the world."

REFLECTION

1. When you get to the heart of the matter, what's in your heart is what really matters.
2. There are three days in your life to celebrate: the day you were born, the day you chose to experience a new birth, and the day you discovered your purpose.
3. *And why are you anxious about clothing? Consider the lilies of the field, how they grow: they neither toil nor spin, yet I tell you, even Solomon in all his glory was not arrayed like one of these.* — Matthew 6:27-28

CHOOSE TO HAVE AN "I CAN DO IT" ATTITUDE

Wake up determined, go to sleep satisfied.
– George Lorimer

I love the classic story of *The Little Engine That Could* by Watty Piper. Every time I read it, I get inspired and gain new insights. To me, it's the story of a little engine that is willing to try something he has never done before, mainly to ascend a steep mountain to help someone.

He could have said, "I can't do this," or "I don't want to do this," or "It's too difficult." However, he chooses to have a positive attitude and say, "I think I can, I think I can, I think I can." And he does it.

As a poor farm boy in rural Wood County, Ohio, back in the '50s, I wanted to go away to college. I had never been far from home so the thought of being 500 miles from my family made me anxious. I had six older brothers and sisters (and one younger), none of which had gone to college. So I had no one to coach me on what to expect or to give me words of encouragement. I had to keep talking to myself and telling myself, "I can do this, I think I can. I think I can."

Even with a desire to go to college, I wasn't sure I would be able to go because of finances. To my surprise, however, my mother told me one day during my senior year in high school that she had saved up enough money for me to go to college. She said we could get through at least the first year and after that we would have to have faith that God would provide. I will be forever grateful to my mother for her gift of love that made it possible.

To be honest, though, I got a little nervous once the financial obstacle was removed. That meant the door was now open to leave the comfort of home and all that was familiar to me and go away to college where everything was unfamiliar and unknown. There was no excuse to stay home. But the reality of leaving family and friends was hitting me. I have to admit there were fleeting moments when I wanted to change my mind and forget about college. But something within me wouldn't let me give up. I kept saying, "I can do this. I can do this." And in 1956, amidst the fabulous '50s, I did go away to college.

My brother, Bob, my mother, and my dear Aunt Blanche, took me to college. We drove from the rural farms of northern Ohio, down old route 25, to the big southern city of Nashville in one day. What a drastic change in scenery, weather, and culture. I felt like I was in another world. In fact, I was.

Bob pulled in front of my dormitory, set my suitcase on the sidewalk, and said they were going to head home. I didn't realize things were going to happen so fast. Part of me wanted to hang onto them and beg them to stay for a few days. I was even tempted to set my dreams aside, jump back in the car, and go home with them. But after hugs and brief farewells, they left....without me.

I stood on the sidewalk and watched them drive out of sight. That was probably the loneliest moment I ever experienced in my life. I was far from home and all that was familiar to me. I was alone in a big city I had never seen before. I was on a college campus I had never visited. I knew no one. I had little money. All I knew was the name of my dormitory and my assigned room number.

You might say I was about to grow up in a hurry. I got to my room, unpacked, took a deep breath, and made a plan of action. I studied a map of the campus layout so I would know where to go to register for classes. I learned where the campus mail boxes were and hoped to soon get a letter from home. Having a connection to home was important to me. Keeping in touch with Muriel, my high school sweetheart, who was still in high school, was also important. I got information about the city's bus system because that was going to be my only mode of transportation. I had to learn where stores were so I could ride the bus there and buy supplies.

I must admit, there were times during the next few weeks when I still thought about packing my suitcase, going to the bus station, and heading for home. But I'm glad I didn't. Going away to college turned out to be one of the best decisions in my life. It afforded me a wide and varied educational experience that enlightened me in so many ways and broadened my horizons. I will always be appreciative of the opportunity that was afforded me.

I'm not sure why, but there's a tendency for people, especially as they get older, to resist change and try new things. There's a tendency to say, "I don't think I can," rather than, "I think I can." There's a tendency to say, "I'm too old to do things like that." But to do so is to miss the many rich experiences that might help you feel vibrant and alive.

The challenge is to live life more creatively by embracing an "I can do it" attitude and trying new things. It's setting goals you would love to accomplish and doing what it takes to make them happen. It's saying, "I think I can." And then saying, "I know I can."

REFLECTION

1. These are my two favorite friends. They help me through a lot of tough times. They are: I Can and I Will.
2. Others can encourage me and give me support, but only I can choose to make the changes I know I need to make. It's up to me. I can do it. And I will.
3. *Let us run with perseverance the race that is marked out for us.* — Hebrews 12:1

THERE'S NO PLACE LIKE HOME

Home is where your story began
— Annie Danielson

When my mother was in the hospital, gravely ill, and in pain, I was holding her hand when she said to me in a soft voice, "I want to go home."

Home and family meant so much to her, and I wish I could have helped her get home one more time. Home was her place of comfort. But it was not to be.

Part of me believes she meant she wanted to let go of life and pain and discomfort and go to her eternal home, the place she often sang about in hymns. If she meant her eternal home, she made it there the next day.

I think there's an ache for home that lives in all of us. We long for that home where our story began, where we first experienced family, where our first memories were created, friendships were first formed, and dreams began.

Home as a youth may not bring forth positive images for everyone, but there's good news knowing that, as adults, we can create the home we want, where we feel comfortable, relaxed, and safe, where we feel a sense of belonging. We can create the home we always want to go back to.

So when in life you wonder which path to take, always take the one that leads home, because no matter where you go in life or how far you choose to roam, there's no place like home.

I remember when I went away to college I got homesick and wished I could go home for a weekend visit, but home was 500 miles away and getting home was out of the question. It was difficult for me to wait until Thanksgiving break to be able to go home. Always a bit short on cash, I had to take the bus home for Thanksgiving instead of flying.

As the bus got closer to my home area, I remember how good it felt to see all the places that were familiar to me and how good it felt to see them. My dad picked me up at the bus station. He wasn't one to be demonstrative with his feelings, but I could tell he was as glad to see me as I was glad to see him.

When we got home, I remember walking into the house and soaking in all the familiarities of home — the aroma of food being prepared for the Thanksgiving meal, the kitchen where the family gathered around the table for meals, the old pantry where we hung our coats, the coal-burning stove in the dining room that made the room warm and cozy, the living room with the old television set sitting on a small table, and, of course, my bedroom upstairs that had been my get-away spot. Most important were the familiar faces of family members with their smiles and hugs. I was home and it felt so good. Humble it was, but I knew there was no place like it.

Later that night when I crawled into bed, I thought about all the things that home meant to me. I made a list in my mind. I fell asleep after getting to number forty on my list. It made me feel good to realize how much home meant to me. Since that time, I have done this little exercise in my mind several times.

I remember when I was working on a graduate degree at Ohio State University, I was swamped with term papers that were due and felt that I couldn't take time to go home for Thanksgiving. We had two young daughters at the time, so my wife, Muriel, said she would take them and drive home to her parents and my parents for the holiday and give me time to finish my papers.

They left and I recall how difficult it was for me to concentrate on getting my papers done. All I could think about was home and family and wonderful food and all the nostalgia that goes with the Thanksgiving holiday. I was feeling a bit down when, much to my surprise, our Latvian neighbor brought over a large plate of their Thanksgiving meal — sauerkraut, boiled potatoes, sausages, creamed corn, and homemade bread. It was such a treat and helped to ease my longing for home. It's amazing what a small act of kindness can do to comfort the soul, especially when you are alone and lonely.

Home is such a special place. For most people, it's where you first experienced being loved. It was your refuge and where you found comfort. It's where your values were formed and, in most cases, still guide your life. Home is where your first memories were etched in your mind, where you connected with friends, and where your first dreams were formed. Everything that meant home to you became engrained in your DNA. It's part of who you are.

There's something so true about that old statement, "Be it ever so humble, there's no place like home."

REFLECTION

1. It's okay to go and seek your dreams, but always remember where your home is.
2. Life will take you to unexpected places, love will bring you home. — Melissa McClone
3. *By wisdom a house is built, and through understanding it is established; through knowledge its rooms are filled with rare and beautiful treasures.* —Proverbs 24:3-4

EMBRACING LIFE'S CHALLENGES

I ain't down yet.

I would like to share some of the journey that my wife, Muriel, and I have taken in recent years and some of the difficult issues we've faced. Through it all, we feel blessed and encouraged. I hope our story will serve as an encouragement to you as well.

There are certain things that people associate with growing older. Health issues. Aches. Pains. Hospitalizations. Physical limitations. Hearing loss. Memory loss. Loss of loved ones. These are the things I call the negatives.

What's interesting is that we can choose how we're going to react to these negatives. We can choose to respond with even more negatives. Discouragement. Anger. Bitterness. Frustration. Hopelessness. Helplessness. Dismay. Defeat. We can make growing older a negative experience.

But we can also choose to react to the negatives with positives. Determination. Hopefulness. Encouragement. Creativeness. Faithfulness. Altruism. We each have what it takes to choose how we're going to react and how we're going to live our life.

Erik Erikson, the renowned developmental psychologist, theorized that humans go through eight stages of life. The eighth and final stage of life is called "ego integrity vs. despair," and begins at approximately age 65. According to Erikson, it's up to us how we embrace this last and final stage of life. We can fill our days with regrets about what we didn't accomplish in life, things we wish we had done but didn't. We can spend time filling our time with regrets about people we wish we had spent more time with. We can regret the things we did do but wish we hadn't. As the result of our regrets and failed dreams, we can live our final stage of life in despair, and say to ourselves, "If only," or "What if."

On the other hand, Erikson says we can choose to embrace this last stage of life and contemplate the things we feel we have accomplished, no matter how small. We can focus on the good we feel we have done and the good times we've had. With what time we have left in life we can look ahead with a sense of joy and dream about what still can be.

I have personally chosen to embrace this eighth and final stage with what Erikson calls "integrity and wisdom." There have been moments of discouragement, and I'm sure there will be more, but I'm determined to face the challenges with courage and a positive outlook. I'm determined to fill my heart with hope and my mind with dreams. I'm determined to make the most of it, perhaps make it the best stage of all. I believe it's possible.

Major health challenges have come my way in the last few years that have put my positive outlook to the test. It hasn't been easy. My faith, my wife, Muriel, and a positive attitude have helped me through the toughest and darkest moments.

With each challenge that I faced over the last few years, I kept telling myself, "I ain't down yet." That's one of my favorite songs and it comes from the movie, *The Unsinkable Molly Brown,* which is a fictionalized account of Margaret Brown's life. She survived the 1912 sinking of the *RMS Titanic a*nd reportedly helped rescue many of the passengers. She faced numerous struggles and rejections in her life. She got knocked down many times, but refused to stay down. She became strong and determined. She spent much of her later years in life advocating for women and the elderly. The song captures her determined spirit.

For some reason, those four words in the song title come to mind as I have gone through my health struggles. With every new diagnosis that I didn't want to hear, I would give myself time to deal with it, then say, "I ain't down yet."

It all started in 2010. I had routine blood work done for my next doctor's appointment. After reviewing my lab report, the doctor said the results showed some abnormalities. He referred me to an oncologist who did further blood tests and diagnosed me with Monoclonal Gammopathy of an Undetermined Significance (MGUS).

The term itself scared me when I first heard it, especially since it deals with a bone marrow problem. I remember standing on the deck on the back of our former house that night after getting the diagnosis. I looked up at the stars and wondered how many more opportunities I would have to enjoy God's amazing universe. How much more time would I have with my family? I guess it's somewhat natural for a person to initially think the worst. I did plenty of that. But after I had my "pity party," I told myself, "I ain't down yet." I was determined to face the facts head-on and make the most of it. I wasn't going to give in or give up.

MGUS is a condition in which an abnormal protein is produced in a type of white blood cell in your bone marrow. It usually causes no significant problems if it remains as MGUS, but can progress to a terminal cancer called multiple myeloma. You have what is commonly called "bad protein spikes" in your bone marrow. The goal is to keep the "spikes" from increasing.

Unfortunately, my "spikes" have increased twice. I am blessed to have an excellent oncologist who keeps the condition monitored and helps me maintain a positive outlook. Never underestimate the importance of having a physician who cares about you and shows it.

Getting unexpected news like this prompted Muriel and me to sit down and discuss our future. We wanted to be prepared for whatever other challenges might occur in our lives. At the time, I was 74 years old and she was 72. We could have gone into denial and not think about it. But we wanted to be proactive and be prepared for whatever else might happen. We decided to explore the possibility of giving up our home and moving into a retirement community. Someone gave us excellent advice, "Do it before you have to." That's what we did.

After exploring different retirement living options, we made the decision to sell our home and move into a nearby active retirement community that we liked. We chose a community that offered independent living as well as assisted living, long-term care, and memory care. We were both relieved to know that we would not be responsible for any maintenance of our home or yard. I wanted the security of knowing that if anything happened to me, Muriel would not have to worry about maintenance and upkeep.

In addition to maintenance, we would have daily access to health services, organized activities, exercise programs, entertainment, transportation, and so much more. What was really important, we would be challenged with daily creative activities that would stimulate our minds and give us purpose. We knew it was important for us to live among active adults. It would give us the opportunity to share mutual interests and experiences and be stimulated by good dialogue and companionship.

I have to say, however, that it was difficult for us to down-size and get rid of things we had collected over the years. It was an emotional experience to let go of many of our favorite possessions. We were pleased that our children were willing to take some of the items and keep the heirlooms in the family.

Not long after we moved into our retirement villa I had another surprise. I was diagnosed with type two diabetes. This is a serious disease, not to be taken lightly. It can contribute to other health problems, such as kidney disease. For example, I learned that I also have stage three kidney failure. It was difficult news to hear.

Diabetes calls for a major change in lifestyle. Muriel had been diagnosed with type two diabetes a few years earlier, so we have been able to work on lifestyle changes together. We have an excellent endocrinologist who closely monitors our diabetes and keeps us on track.

On one of our visits to our endocrinologist in 2015, he noticed what sounded like a murmur in my heart. He referred me to my family physician, who then referred me to a cardiologist. After a series of tests, the cardiologist diagnosed me with pulmonary hypertension. My family physician, however, didn't think I had pulmonary hypertension. After extensive research on the internet about the disease, I agreed with my family physician. It didn't seem to be what I had. So I decided to get a second opinion.

I went to the Mayo Clinic in Jacksonville, Florida. After two days of tests, the team of doctors there concluded that I did not have pulmonary hypertension, but I did have hypertrophic cardiomyopathy. It's possibly a genetic disease. The heart muscle becomes abnormally thick without any apparent cause. It results in the heart being less able to pump blood effectively. It tends to cause shortness of breath and an irregular heartbeat. It's a condition that can cause sudden cardiac arrest, sometimes associated with the sudden deaths of young athletes. This was news that took me by surprise and got me to thinking seriously about my own mortality. Life suddenly seemed a bit more fragile. But I kept telling myself, "I ain't down yet." I was determined to stay positive.

A year later, Muriel and I traveled to Ohio to visit relatives. During the trip I was not feeling well. By the time I got to Ohio I was feeling worse. When we got to the city where her sister lived, we went straight to an urgent care facility. The medical staff took X-rays and referred me to the local hospital where I was diagnosed with a serious case of pneumonia. They admitted me to ICU, mainly because of my heart condition. Fortunately, recovery went well. After getting out of the hospital four days later and feeling well enough to travel, we returned to Florida.

Still not feeling well when we returned home, I again made an appointment at the Mayo Clinic. While there I was diagnosed with bronchiecstasis. It's a condition where the bronchial tubes of your lungs are permanently damaged, widened and thickened. This allows bacteria and mucus to build up and pool in your lungs. The result is frequent infections and airway blockages. It often gets worse over time and can be fatal. I use a nebulizer to take treatments at home. My pulmonologist keeps my condition monitored. Fortunately it seems to keep things under control, at least for the present time. As I sit there doing the treatment, I remind myself how blessed I am to be alive. I tell myself, "I ain't down yet."

Just when I thought everything was going well and under control, my cardiologist ordered an echocardiogram. The result showed that the aortic valve in my heart was not functioning correctly. It's a condition where the valve doesn't close tightly and some of the blood regurgitates and leaks back into the heart. This requires the heart to pump harder, which over time can lead to heart failure. My heart condition was considered to be in a moderate to severe status. Another echocardiogram was ordered so the two results could be compared. The second echocardiogram confirmed what the first one showed. The aortic valve was defective. The cardiologist recommended a "wait and see" approach until another echocardiogram could be done at a later date. I'm not comfortable with a "wait and see" approach but yielded to the wisdom of the cardiologist. She is very caring and professional and I trust her judgment.

I must admit, I started to wonder if there was more bad news to come. I didn't like the track record I was creating. This last news hit me hard and sort of knocked me to my knees. But I kept telling myself to be positive, to appreciate my blessings. I was determined to stand up and keep fighting, keep functioning, and refuse to give up. Again, I reminded myself, "I ain't down yet."

In between my trips to the Mayo Clinic, Muriel had her own medical struggles. Thirty-five years earlier, she had severely broken her ankle and has worn a brace ever since to help her walk. Unfortunately, the condition of her ankle seemed to be deteriorating. After meeting with an orthopedic surgeon, it was decided that her ankle needed repair work. He took out screws and put new ones in and did an excellent job of stabilizing her ankle. However, not long after surgery, she broke her tibia bone. This proved to be a very painful break and required her to be in a wheel chair. Eight months later, we discovered that the tibia break was not healing. To correct the problem, the surgeon had to put in a rod, screws and a metal plate. This meant more months of non-weight bearing and staying in a wheelchair.

Through all of this, Muriel and I have worked hard to stay upbeat. In spite of our health issues, we're determined to enjoy our older years as creatively as possible. Rather than focus on limitations and what we can't do, we focus on possibilities and making dreams come true. We focus on the positives.

Muriel joined two choirs on campus and enjoys the rehearsals and the concerts. She recently played a role in a Christmas comedy. As a former trombone player, she also decided to buy a trombone and start practicing again. Her "lip" came back quickly, and on one occasion she performed a solo as part of a choir concert and also performed in a talent show. She keeps busy crocheting, sewing, and playing the piano, among many other creative activities. She recently discovered a new hobby: making old-fashioned button dolls. Much of what she makes she enjoys giving away as gifts to others. She loves to bring joy to others.

Having both been raised on farms, we like having fresh vegetables from the garden. So we designed and built a raised-bed vegetable garden on the one side of our villa. It's large enough to provide us with a variety of fresh vegetables but small enough for us to maintain without it becoming overwhelming. We built a bench and placed it beside the vegetable garden to sit and watch our vegetables grow. All of these projects were good for us and kept us focused on the positives. They involved some creative thinking and were fun to do.

My time over the past two years has been spent writing and oil painting. I've enjoyed having the time to write. I've written a fairly large volume of literature, including poems, short stories, children's picture books, middle grade and young adult novels, and some non-fiction. I was pleased that one of my short stories was published in the 2019 Chicken Soup for the Soul

Christmas Edition, "It's Beginning to Look a Lot like Christmas." It was encouraging to me.

My goal has not been to focus on publishing as much as it has been to simply enjoy creative expression and experience the joy of writing. Overall, the writing has been a wonderful period of reflection for me and in its own way has been therapeutic and healing.

One of the highlights during this period was to write the lyrics to a song titled, "Who Do You See in the Manger?" My son in Chicago, who was a music major in college, composed the music. His wife, who got her master's in opera, did the vocal. They both did an excellent job of making my lyrics sound good. It turned out to be a creative family project and lots of fun to do. Having created one song, we were inspired to begin working on an Irish lullaby for children. (See the lyrics to the songs in the appendix.)

Another writing project that has been a real challenge to me is my blog. I write a brief blog each day and post it online. It's a great way for me to start my day. It stimulates my mind and helps me think positive and encouraging thoughts. I recently put the blog on hold until I got this book finished.

Oil painting has also been a great opportunity for me to express myself creatively. I must admit that I haven't discovered my niche, though. I paint all kinds of subjects, from landscapes, to portraits, to flowers, to birds, to art deco, and more. I've enjoyed the freedom to paint what I'm in the mood to explore on any given day. I've tried to paint on a somewhat regular basis and learn as I go. I'm a self-taught painter and realize I have a lot to learn. Thus far I have had the privilege of conducting one art show. And like the writing process, painting has been therapeutic and healing.

It's funny how feeling a little confident in one thing can inspire you to try something else. Enjoying the oil painting has helped me to stretch and try pen and ink sketches, watercolor paintings, and even pastels. It has been a fun experience and I have enjoyed the opportunity to explore and grow.

Muriel and I have fully embraced this last stage of our life and have discovered a variety of ways to enjoy it creatively. Through it all, we have been able to maintain a positive outlook on life and we're both determined to make the most of each day.

We get up each morning and the first thing we do is give thanks for life and the opportunity we have to enjoy another day. Starting our day by being grateful sets a positive tone for the rest of the day. We're determined to enjoy life and "live happily ever after." "We ain't down yet."

REFLECTION

1. Never live in fear and run from challenges and struggles. Rather, run toward them determined to experience the joy of victory. Choose joy over fear.
2. Believe in yourself. What is within you is greater than any obstacle outside you.
3. *We are hard pressed on every side but not crushed, perplexed, but not in despair, pursued but not abandoned, knocked down but not defeated.* — 2 Corinthians 4:8-9

WHAT REALLY MATTERS IN LIFE

There's a time to keep and a time to throw away.
— Ecclesiastes 3·6

My wife, Muriel, and I live in a two-bedroom villa in a retirement community in Tallahassee and have spent many hours turning the backyard into our own personal retreat. It's something we can enjoy without having to go somewhere else to find a place of respite. It's there for us to enjoy every day and we do. We have put a great deal of creative expression into the yard to make it "our own little paradise."

In one corner just outside our sunroom is my "meditation garden." It has a bench, water cascading over rocks, flowers, a statue of St. Francis of Assisi, and looks out over our bird feeders and the wooded area behind our villa. I often sit there in the early morning with my cup of coffee, listen to the birds as they awaken and sing, and reflect on life.

By the way, let me put in a plug for meditation. Even in its simplest form, it can have both physiological and psychological effects. While experts don't fully understand how meditation works, research clearly demonstrates that it can have a range of positive effects on overall health.

Muriel has her own meditation spot. She has created what she calls her "secret garden" in the front of the villa, just outside our screened-in porch. She has two fountains with soft trickling water, a beautiful Greek statue that she calls "Rachel," a picket fence with a honeysuckle vine, and a variety of plants and flowers. In the porch, she has a swing that we built, to sit in and enjoy her garden.

We both find that these favorite spots of ours give us moments of peace and relaxation. They make it easy to put the busy world aside, reflect for a few moments, and enjoy the beauty and sounds of nature. Although we enjoy our separate gardens, we often sit together in the porch in the early morning hours or early evening hours; look out over her secret garden, and chat.

Our son, Denver, who lives in Tallahassee and is knowledgeable about technology and is gifted at construction, has added lighting and special effects in Muriel's secret garden, my meditation garden, the patio and the wooded area behind our home. He even created an old fashioned lantern that looks like a gas light at the entrance to our driveway. It's creative and sets a nice mood. And the good news is that it's all on timers. Everything works automatically. He has made it easy for us to enjoy.

By the way, if you haven't created your own special retreat setting, I highly recommend it. I think everyone needs a place, no matter how small, where they can get away from the busyness of the world and take the time to sit and reflect. It doesn't have to be elaborate. A comfortable chair in a place where you can have privacy is adequate.

As I was sitting on my bench one morning, I thought about how life can get so complicated and busy that it's easy to lose sight of what's really important. It got me to thinking about what really matters in life. What is it that gives meaning to life and is important for people to experience?

As an older adult, I've seen many things in life that I think really matter. I've also counseled with many individuals over the years and have heard from them the things that made a difference in their lives. As I sat on the bench and thought about what it was that mattered in life, I decided that I would come up with my own list.

It turned out to be a thought-provoking experience. It's something I recommend for others to do as well. It forced me to sort through and examine my values, interests, and priorities. It also forced me to reflect on my purpose in life and think about why I'm here.

I keep my list and reflect on it from time to time. I've made a few adjustments to it over the years and that's what is interesting about life. Things change. So it's important to be willing to change and not be afraid to make adjustments as needed.

I would like to share my list with you. I hope you will read it and create your own. Here's what matters to me:

SELF
Believe in yourself. Love yourself. Be kind to yourself. Look in the mirror and tell yourself you are valuable and lovable and that you have worth as a person. Before going to bed each night, remind yourself of at least one thing you have to offer the world, no matter how small. (A smile is a good example.). Accept the fact that you have abilities and are capable of doing something of worth because good things are within you. Take time to discover and nurture them. Be real. Be genuine. Don't try to be who you are not. Always be who you are. It takes less energy.

RELATIONSHIPS
An effective relationship is based on one powerful principle: do for the other person what you would want that person to do for you. It's as much about giving as it is receiving. It's as much about being able to express yourself effectively as it is about learning to listen well. It's as much about enjoying what you have in common as it is about respecting your differences. It's not about finding someone who will complete you, it's about finding someone who will love and accept you for who you are. Never allow someone to try and change you to be who they want you to be. In every relationship, choose to be an encourager instead of a critic. Encouragement draws people together, criticism separates them. And remember, neglect kills a relationship. It grows when you take the time to nourish it and help each other be a better person.

FOCUS
It's important to be realistic about life. It's not going to last forever. There will come a time when you will see no more sunrises, no more sunsets, and no more tomorrows. So make the most of every day. Focus on the things you consider to be important in your life, such as people—family, and friends. Connect with them as often as possible. Tell them more about *whom* you are as a person

and less about *what* you do in life. Be transparent. Leave them with memories of the real you — your hopes, your dreams, your failures, your victories, all the things that make you who you are. Share with them what matters to you.

OPPORTUNITIES

Make sure you have dreams in life. But don't just have them. Go after all the things you want to do in life while there's still an opportunity to do so. For when life expires, all the things you left undone will expire as well. The world is full of unfinished symphonies that will never get played, unfinished projects that will never get completed, unfinished books that will never get read or written, and trips that will never get taken. So pursue what's important to you. Seize opportunities before they slip away. Don't delay—do it! Carpe Diem!

GIVING

Spend more time giving in life and less time receiving, more time sharing and less time buying, more time participating and less time observing. People will remember you by what you gave in life, what you built, what you contributed, not by what you owned or what you acquired in life. Be generous with your gift of time and with your love.

EXAMPLE

Live your life in such a way that others will want to follow your example. Show compassion for others, especially the less fortunate. Be willing to make sacrifices in order to help those in need. Demonstrate honesty and integrity in all you do. Look for ways to encourage and inspire those who need a lift in life. And when you love, don't just say it—show your love—and show it unconditionally. Accept others for who they are and where they are in life.

TIME

Spend more time on what is good in life, the positives, the little things that mean a lot, things that touch the heart and inspire. Spend more time with the people you love. Reach out to them. Let them know you care. With all the communication devices available to us, there's no excuse not to be in touch. Spend less time on the negatives, the wrongs, the trivial, and the things that don't really matter. Time is a precious gift. Be wise about how you use it. Make it count.

FORGIVENESS

Determine whom you need to forgive and then do it. Let go of the pain they have caused you. It will help you heal. Don't carry hurts, resentments, anger, and jealousies around with you, day after day. They become a heavy burden. Write them down on a piece of paper and then destroy the paper and let go. Be free of the burdens. Clear the air and rest in peace. Remember, forgiveness doesn't mean you accept what someone has done to hurt you, rather it means you are no longer going to let it affect your life. You're going to let go. And for those individuals you may have hurt over the years, find some way to communicate your regrets to them. If you don't know where they are or they have passed on, you can still write a letter to express your thoughts and feelings, and then destroy it. Let go of it.

CHOICES

No matter your situation, you always have choices in life. Having a choice is a freedom that was given in the beginning of time. It's inherent in every human being, and no one can take it away from you unless you allow it. But be wise in what you choose in life. Choose what is healthy. Choose the things that help you grow as a person, not the things that hurt and hinder you. And remember, you always have the right to say no.

HEALTH

Take care of your mind, body, and soul. Feed them wisely with good nourishment. Be disciplined and exercise mentally, physically, and spiritually on a consistent basis. Develop healthy relationships. Surround yourself with people who encourage you and build you up. Exclude or avoid those who demean you. Take time to reflect, meditate, and pray.

WORK

Work matters. When possible, choose work that allows you to express who you are as a person, your interests, values, and abilities. The best work is that which you love to do. It's meaningful to you. You feel productive in doing it. It gives you a sense of satisfaction. When work feels like just a job to you, there's something you can do. Consider having a hobby or avocation that will help give your life balance and allow you to express your interests and abilities. Whatever you do, give it your best effort. There's satisfaction and pride in knowing that you have done a good job.

VISION

Faith is an important part of vision. It's believing that all things are possible. It's unseen but felt. It's strength when you feel you have none, hope when all seems lost. It's what helps you to never give up. It's having a vision of what can be. It empowers you to fill your heart with hope and your mind with dreams. Never stop dreaming and never stop believing. Always reach beyond where you are. Have the courage to reach high and reach far.

As I created my list, I was surprised at how it gave me a clear picture of what's important to me. It helped me sort out my purpose in life. I can get up each day and realize I have a personalized plan for living, a basic belief system to guide me through my day. It has helped me look beyond my health issues and realize I have a lot to live for. It helps me stay focused on the positives. It reminds me that "I ain't down yet."

REFLECTION

1. At the end of life, what really matters is not your position in life or what you've accumulated, but the positive impact you made on others.
2. What's important in life is being content to make do with what you have.
3. *Whatever is true, whatever is noble, whatever is right, whatever is pure, whatever is lovely, whatever is admirable — if anything is excellent or praiseworthy — think about such things.* —Philippians 4:8

THERE'S SOMETHING SPIRITUAL ABOUT NATURE

Never stop attending nature's magnificent classroom.

I love nature. On many mornings, even chilly ones, I get my cup of coffee, go outside, sit on the bench in my meditation garden, and quietly observe nature. Every time I sit there and admire the perfection, the balance, the harmony, the diversity that surrounds me, I am awed. To me, it's a profound spiritual experience.

When I say spiritual, I mean nature touches my inner being. It touches the spirit within me. It's not something that can easily be put into words. All I know is that the nature I love is both instructional and inspiring. When I sit and observe, I learn. When I sit and listen, I hear music. If I'm patient, I always see a sermon, short and reflective. Yesterday I watched a sermon on the topic, "It's more blessed to give than to receive." Mr. Cardinal took seeds from the bird feeder, flew to Mrs. Cardinal, and fed her. What a beautiful message of love and giving.

The lessons from nature are endless. The key is to observe with a watchful eye, to look and listen creatively at what's going on, because often the smallest, most minute object will teach an insightful lesson. It may be how a seed emerges from the soil, how a squirrel finds an acorn, how a leaf miner curls a leaf, or how a wren builds a nest in less than an hour. The teachings are infinite.

My daughter, Luanne, who lives in Loveland, Ohio (Cincinnati), has a beautiful backyard filled with flowers and plants in every corner. She and her husband, John, have worked hard to construct flower beds and special boxes for growing vegetables. John is excellent at construction and Luanne does a great job of knowing what to put where. Their creative expression is evident throughout the yard. Luanne enjoys her early morning stroll with coffee in hand. It's a joy for her to watch things grow. Every day, nature offers something new to appreciate.

Without question, nature is the world's greatest classroom. It's in this classroom that we learn not only about nature but about life itself. The teachings are spiritual and profound. There's a divineness that is mysteriously present. If you allow it, it will touch you deeply.

REFLECTION

1. All the amazing mysteries of life are found in nature.
2. The human spirit is encouraged by discovering nature's hidden beauty not yet altered by the hands of man.
3. *He has made everything beautiful in its time.* —Ecclesiastes 3:11

A WORM TAUGHT ME A LESSON

Even the snail made it to the ark.
— Charles Spurgeon

One warm summer day I was outside and noticed an earthworm crawling across our driveway.

I stopped and looked at it. What a persistent worm, I thought. The sun was pounding the driveway with sweltering summer heat, making the cement hot and dry. But the worm crawled anyway. It didn't seem to hesitate at all. Inch by inch it moved forward.

It could have waited until the cool of night, but it chose to not delay. This worm was not about to put off till tomorrow what it could do today. I was awed by its determination to get to the other side of the driveway. I admired its effort and wondered what it would be like if everyone, including myself, had such resolve, such willpower.

I watched the worm go in a straight line, not wavering, not halting, and not giving up. It had a rhythm, a slow constant movement that moved it closer and closer to its goal. I wondered if the discipline was innate or if the worm had a mother and father who taught it the value of order and control.

I needed the lesson the worm taught me as it crawled across our driveway. There were things I needed to get done, things I had put off. After watching the worm, I knew it wouldn't be right to come up with more excuses and delay the tasks I needed to do. I decided to get to work.

Never would I have thought that a tiny worm could teach me an important lesson about life. But it taught me well — one of the best sermons I ever saw.

Nature is an amazing classroom. We can read many books filled with knowledge and inspiration, attend hundreds of classes and seminars, sit at the feet of renowned teachers, but our most profound learning will come from nature. There is only one requirement. We must be open to discovering. Many of the world's greatest thinkers found their inspiration in nature.

Too often we fail to take advantage of what nature offers. One day while I was sitting on the bench in my meditation garden, I thought about all the things that nature teaches us. In just a few minutes I came up with a list. Here are just a few of the things I believe nature teaches us:

1. It shows us the mystery and the wonder of the cycle of life.
2. It reminds us that wonder, amazement, and awe still exist without the help of technology.
3. When surrounded by nature, we learn how to let go of the stress and worries that overwhelm us and give ourselves permission to be grounded in the present moment.
4. It teaches us the value of simplicity and the joy of being content with what we have. There is no need to have the latest product. The simplicity of nature suffices. Nature makes do with what it has.
5. It teaches us to be strong and persevere. After the ravages of forest fires, tornadoes, hurricanes, and other natural disasters, nature survives and often comes back stronger than before.
6. We learn that every form of beauty is found in nature and it's all natural.

REFLECTION

1. Success is often achieved not by strength but by perseverance.
2. Ordinary people reach difficult goals with extraordinary determination.
3. At *the proper time, we will reap a harvest of blessings if we don't give up.* —Galatians 6:9

SOMETIMES IT'S OKAY TO ACT A LITTLE SQUIRRELY

Life is better when you lighten up.

I admit that I have a love-hate relationship with squirrels. Some days they're cute and funny. Other days they are a nuisance as they attack our bird feeders or wreak havoc in our vegetable garden. Believe it or not, squirrels eat our spinach, collard greens and beet tops. Trust me, I know. I guess that's why they're all so healthy.

Most days they are just plain squirrely — jumpy, nutty, flighty, unpredictable — scurrying around in a mildly insane manner.

Let me confess something. The other day when I was scurrying around, being flighty, acting a little nutty, maybe behaving mildly insane, like I do on occasion, I thought, "Just look at me. I'm acting squirrely." My dad had another name for it. He called it "acting like a chicken with its head cut off."

But you know what? Sometimes it's okay. There's no reason to fret about it or be concerned. That's who I am sometimes. Every once in a while I give myself permission to be a little crazy, to act a little squirrely.

Actually there are benefits to acting a little silly and having a good laugh. It contributes positively to one's overall well-being. Laughter is good for you.

Here's something everyone needs to know. Research suggests that laughter has benefits:

- It triggers the release of endorphins, our feel-good hormone. Laughing makes you feel good.
- It promotes bonding and draws people closer together.

- It protects one's heart.
- It increases brain activity.

Unfortunately it's often not easy for adults to let loose and act silly. It's hard for them to let go and lighten up. It goes against what they've been conditioned to believe is standard adult behavior. I believe we've forgotten about the "little kid" inside of us that likes to have fun. Maybe it's time to give the little kid permission to act a bit squirrely.

The next time you feel like acting a little squirrely, go right ahead and be silly. It's good for you. Be as creative as you can in acting squirrely. Make your silly time fun and unique.

As frustrated as I sometimes get with squirrels, they often do make me laugh. One squirrel in particular has made me laugh a lot. I call him Loony Leaping Leo. In his mind, I believe he thinks he can fly. He tries and fails, but he keeps trying. I admire his tenacity.

Leo's antics take place just outside our sunroom. We have two bird feeders in our flower bed. They are on poles, each with several baffles to keep the squirrels and raccoons from climbing the poles and getting the bird seed. The bird feeders are at one end of the flower bed. At the other end of the flower bed, about 12 feet away, is another pole with hanging plants on it.

Leo desperately wants to get to the bird seed. I can tell that he wants that bird seed more than anything in the whole wide world. The problem is he can't get past the baffles. But it doesn't keep him from trying. One day he figured he would climb the pole with the hanging plants and try to leap the 12 feet to the bird feeders. I watched him climb the pole, survey the situation, hesitate for a moment, then launch toward the bird feeders. Loony Leaping Leo almost made it. Almost. Unfortunately for him, he hit the bird feeder pole head on.....smack! He fell to the ground, half dazed, and perhaps with a slight brain concussion. Did he give up? No.

He went back to the hanging plant pole and climbed it. This time he took longer to survey the situation. He steadied himself atop the pole. Then, with his eyes still glazed from the first head-on endeavor, he launched another super squirrel leap. Another crash. Another failure. Refusing to admit himself to the nearest animal hospital, he dusted himself off, un-crossed his eyes, and went back to the hanging plant pole. He was not going to give up.

After his eighth try, I could no longer watch Leo keep hurting himself. I chased him away and hoped he would go somewhere and recover. Maybe make an appointment for squirrel therapy.

As I later thought about it, I concluded that Leo was just being a determined squirrel. And he was having fun. After each crash, I could almost hear him saying, "I ain't down yet."

It was easy for me to identify with his tenacious attitude, his risk-taking, and his determination to achieve his goal. I remembered the times I leaped far to grasp goals, some of which were out of reach, But, like Leo, I didn't give up. I may have "hit my head against a brick wall" (instead of a pole) many times, but I found ways to get around the wall or over it. Like Leo, I kept telling myself, "I ain't down yet." I kept going and eventually reached many of my goals. And I had fun doing it. It helped to sometimes be a little squirrely.

REFLECTION

1. Lighten up and take the time to laugh. Consider it one of the best forms of therapy.
2. The most boring thing you can do is take yourself too seriously and not accept your own need to lighten up and laugh.
3. *We were filled with laughter and we sang for joy.* —Psalm 126:2

HAVE THE COURAGE TO TURN THE PAGE

You achieve in life what you have the courage to go after.

It's easy and too common for people to reach a certain age and get stuck on one page in life, hesitant to turn the page and move on. Torn between turning the page and closing the book, many choose to close the book and live as if life is over, as if "that's all she wrote."

However, there comes a day when some people realize that perhaps hope is on the next page. They realize that something exciting and interesting awaits them, so they find the courage to turn the page. It's then that they realize turning the page is the best feeling in the world. They discover there is so much more to the book than the page they were stuck on.

My daughter, son-in-law, and their two small children were living in Nevada, near Tahoe, when they decided they wanted to get off the page they were on, turn the page in their life, and write a new chapter of adventure filled with many unknowns. It took a lot of courage. It meant selling their home and everything they owned (except what they put in storage). It meant buying a 55 foot catamaran, leaving their jobs, home-schooling their children, and setting sail on the high seas for over three years. The good news is that they all enjoyed the experience. At the end of the four years, they decided to turn yet another page in their book. They moved to New Zealand to live and are now citizens there.

After 25 years in higher education, Muriel and I decided to turn the page and try something new. After much discussion and prayer we decided to leave northwest Ohio and move to Miami, Florida. It wasn't an easy decision because it meant leaving family and friends and all that was familiar to us. It meant beginning a new venture full of unknowns. It meant taking our youngest son out of the elementary school he was attending and placing him in a new school in a new state and a new environment. It took a lot of courage. Fortunately, it turned out to be a good move.

My ancestor, Ezra Meeker, was a farmer, a gentleman, a civic leader, an author, and a reviled old coot. He was born in Ohio in 1830. In 1852, Ezra and his wife, Eliza, decided to turn the page they were on. They left the comfort of their home and joined thousands of pioneers in the migration west via the Oregon Trail. They settled in the fertile Puyallup Valley in 1862 and later helped found the city of Puyallup. He began raising hops which soon made him a wealthy man. He became known as the "Hop King of the World."

Ezra decided to turn another page in his life and made it his goal to preserve the Oregon Trail. He dedicated the last 20 years of his life in doing just that. He wanted to erect monuments along the trail. In 1905, when he was 75 years old, to help draw attention to his project, he fitted an old covered wagon with two oxen and a driver. He set out on the trail, driving the ox team to the White House in Washington, D.C., where he met with President Teddy Roosevelt. President Roosevelt promised he would ask Congress for money to mark the trail.

In subsequent trips to Washington, D.C., Ezra met with President Woodrow Wilson and President Calvin Coolidge to get their support for preserving the Oregon Trail. He refused to give up on his dream to preserve the trail and set markers.

Don't remain stuck on one page in your book of life if you wish you could move on. Don't remain there if it prevents you from achieving your dreams. Have the courage to turn the page. It will be the first page of the rest of your life, a whole new chapter to enjoy, a new adventure for you to embrace. Turn the page and begin writing. It's never too late.

REFLECTION

1. Believe in yourself. If you have the courage to start something new, you'll be strong enough to finish.
2. Courage is choosing to begin something you've never tried before without any guarantee that you will succeed.
3. *Rise up....take courage and do it!* —Ezra 10:4

GIVE YOURSELF PERMISSION TO BLOOM

Being a late bloomer is better than not blooming at all.

We have a large wooded backyard in the retirement village where we live in north Tallahassee. It's filled with azaleas, sago palms, hydrangeas, and a variety of hollies, among other plants. During the summer months, flowers bloom abundantly.

One very late autumn day, when flowers were no longer blooming, I took a stroll around the yard with a cup of coffee in hand. What a surprise I got when among the dried stems I saw a single purple coneflower standing tall and blooming.

It made me think about life and how it's never too late to bloom. It's perfectly okay to be a late bloomer. Sadly, some people go through life and never bloom. So to bloom at all, even late in life, is something remarkable.

Though you may be in the "late autumn" of your life, or "early winter," there's still time to bloom. My mother-in-law was a late bloomer. She and my father-in-law lived on a farm and raised five children. At age 52, she decided she wanted to go to nursing school. She applied and was accepted. She studied hard and eventually finished the program and graduated with honors. As a result, as an older adult, she accomplished something very important to her.

Perhaps one of the greatest examples and most familiar late bloomers was Anna Mary Robertson Moses, better known as Grandma Moses. She lived on a farm as a child and also when she got married. She didn't start painting until she was in her 70s. An art collector discovered some of her paintings in a local store in 1938 when Grandma Moses was 78. She continued to paint rural settings and became one of the most famous folk artists of the 20th Century.

Give yourself permission and start blooming. Be creative. It's never too late.

REFLECTION

1. The last to bloom is often the one best remembered.
2. Don't stay tight in the bud. Even if it's late in life, allow yourself to unfold and blossom. Let people see how beautiful you are.
3. *Consider the lilies of the field, how they grow; they toil not, neither do they spin: yet I say unto you, that even Solomon in all his glory was not arrayed like one of these.* —Matthew 6:28-29

THE AMAZING POWER
OF KINDNESS

It is more blessed to give than to receive.
— Acts 20·35

One morning, my wife and I had breakfast at a local restaurant. For some reason, we were both a little down. As we were eating I noticed a small, elderly lady sitting alone by the window. Once in a while she would look over at us and smile. What a sweet lady, I thought. She's probably lonely.

She finished eating before we did, and when she walked past us she smiled again. I wondered about her. Was she single? Married? A widow? Did she live alone? Did she have children who lived nearby, or did they live far away? Did she have grandchildren, and did they come to visit her? Was she on a meager income and hardly able to get by?

She left the restaurant and I'll never know the answers to my questions. I'll just know her as a sweet lady, a stranger who sat by the window and who, for some reason, looked at us and smiled.

We finished eating and I asked our server for our check.

"Your meal is paid for," the server said. "That lady who just left paid for your meal."

My wife and I were stunned. What a gracious act of kindness, we thought, and done anonymously. It was a complete surprise. And it's funny how it warmed our hearts, lifted our spirits, and brightened our outlook for the day.

That's what an act of kindness can do. It has the power to change a person's day for the better. I've heard it said, and it's true, that we never rise higher than when we lift another person with an act of kindness.

That was several years ago, and I'm older now, and I tend to forget things on a regular basis, but I don't think I'll ever forget that sweet elderly lady, her gentle smile, and her act of kindness.

A random act of kindness is a non-premeditated action designed to offer kindness towards others. The phrase "practice random kindness and senseless acts of beauty" was written by Anne Herbert on a placemat in Sausalito, California, in 1982. It was based on the phrase, "random acts of violence and senseless acts of cruelty." Herbert's book, *Random Kindness and Senseless Acts of Beauty* was published in 1993 and tells true stories about acts of kindness.

A Chicago man, Ryan Garcia, gained a significant following after doing a different random act of kindness each day of the year in 2012. His 366 random acts spun off into a mission to do an act of kindness in all 50 states in order to raise awareness of deletion syndrome, a disorder caused by a chromosome defect and can cause heart defects, a poor immune system function, cleft palate, and low levels of calcium.

My sister-in-law, Nikki, wanted to complete a random act of kindness that would be easy for her to facilitate since she is limited mobility-wise. She lives near a bus stop. She decided to buy two pairs of shoes and leave them on the bench at the bus stop. It worked. According to the bus driver who observed what happened, the shoes were discovered by individuals who needed shoes. They were pleasantly surprised to find brand new shoes on the bench still in the box.

There's no such thing as a small act of kindness. Every random act of kindness has a significant impact on the recipient's well-being.

The creative aspect to this is to use your imagination to think about the different ways you can do a random act of kindness.....or any kindness at all. The sky's the limit and so are the benefits.

REFLECTION

1. The most effective bridge builder in the world is kindness.
2. Kindness is more than deeds. It's anything that lifts another person and gives them a boost.
3. *Be kind and compassionate to one another.* —Ephesians 4:32

WHAT DOES IT MEAN TO SAY, "HAVE A NICE DAY?"

May your day be bright, your joy be great,
and your cup overflow with love.

How many times during the day do you hear someone say to you, "Have a nice day?" I hear it often, maybe 5 or 6 times a day.

A few days ago I heard it at least 5 times before noon. I heard it at the grocery store, the garden center, from a neighbor, and twice on the phone from friends. I know people mean well when they say it, but what do they mean by it? They probably say it out of habit and don't really think much about it.

Anyway, it got me to thinking. I'm one of those people who wonders about things. I'm always curious about traditions and rituals and how they get started. I like to know why certain things are said or done. So I did a little research.

Here's what I found. The phrase, "Have a nice day," and it's variant, "Have a good day," are commonly spoken expressions used to conclude a conversation or end a message by hoping the person to whom it is addressed experiences a pleasant day. The phrases are typically used by service employees or clerks to customers at the end of a transaction as a way of saying, "Thank you for shopping with us," or "Thank you for using our service."

I was surprised to learn that the phrase came into being as early as 1920, but didn't become widely used until the 1950s. By around 2000, it became a common synonym of the parting phrase, "Goodbye." No one seems to know exactly how or why. It just evolved.

Another variant of the phrase, "Have a good one," supposedly originated in the 1970s by drug addicts who took and sold LSD. The phrase was used to wish the person taking the drug to "have a good trip." Therefore the phrase "have a good one" was used to avoid drawing attention to what you were talking about.

I don't know how accurate the history is or what was originally meant by the phrase, but here's what I do know. When someone wishes you to "have a nice day," they have no control over how your day will go. But you do. Only you can make sure you have a nice day. It's in your hands.

There's one thing I do to make sure I have a nice day. For the most part, it works well. As soon as I wake up each day, I give thanks that I'm alive. After giving thanks, I tell myself why I'm grateful to be alive. It sounds simple, maybe a little crazy, but starting my morning with gratitude sets a positive tone for my whole day. It makes a difference.

So, in ending this communication, here's my wish for you: "Have a nice day."

REFLECTION

1. Each new day is like someone has placed interesting gifts at your door for you to open and enjoy.
2. Though you may fall, you may also rise; though you may fail, you may also succeed; though you may bend and break, you may also overcome and heal. Despite difficult times, you have the power to make the day a good one.
3. *This is the day the Lord has made, rejoice and be glad in it.* —Psalm 118:24

THE TALE OF A GRATEFUL WHALE

In all things give thanks.
– I Thessalonians 5:18

In 2005 a whale made worldwide news. Maybe in part because it was one of those stories that was real, yet it seemed like a fairytale. It appealed to everyone. It had drama, suspense, and compassion

Because of strong appeal, I would like to share the story. In doing so, I would like to give the whale a name because I think she deserves it. She deserves to be called something other than "the whale," or "it." And for some reason the name Dora seems to fit. So this is the story about Dora, a valiant, adorable, grateful whale.

But before I share Dora's story, I would like to briefly comment on humpback whales. They are beautiful, graceful creatures that can grow up to 50 to 60 feet long and weigh up to 40 tons. It's believed they live to be up to 80 years old.

Contrary to what people think, they don't have a hump on their backs. The name comes from the large hump that forms when they arch their backs before making a deep dive into the ocean. Propelling themselves above the water and then splashing back down is called breaching.

Humpback whales are known for their haunting songs, which are sequences of moans, howls, and cries that often continue for hours. Only male whales sing and all males sing the same song. I guess, like humans, once they know the song they can't get it out of their head. Their song can be heard 20 miles away.

Unfortunately, they were almost wiped out in the 20th century by whaling. For years they were relentlessly hunted and slaughtered. In the late 1950s there were only an estimated 440 western South Atlantic humpbacks left. The humpback whales faced extinction.

Fortunately, protections were put in place in the 1960s. Whaling was finally stopped for good in the 1970s. As a result, the humpback population increased to an estimated 25,000. This is an example that if the right things are done environmentally, it can have a positive effect. Nature can recover.

Dora was a young female humpback whale approximately 25 feet long. Like all whales, she loved to play. She could raise high out of the water and then land with a large splash. But one day she became entangled in a spider-like web of nylon crab-trap lines (commercial fisheries gear) off the coast of San Francisco, California. The fishing gear weighed hundreds of pounds.

The entanglement caused Dora to drag the heavy equipment wherever she went. She struggled to free herself of the ropes. The more Dora struggled to get free, the more entangled she became. About twenty crab-trap ropes over two hundred feet long became wrapped around her tail, her back flipper, and even her front flipper. There was even a line caught in her mouth. The ropes cut deep into her flesh.

She fought valiantly to free herself but to no avail. The weight of the ropes pulled her down, forcing her to struggle to keep her blow-hole out of the water. She could barely stay afloat. Dora was in danger of dying.

A crab fisherman spotted the whale struggling in the water and radioed an environmental group for help. After a few hours, a rescue team arrived and, after evaluating the situation, concluded that the whale was so entangled, so caught up in the maze of lines, that it would be almost impossible to free her. They decided that the only way to save her would be to dive in and attempt to untangle her by cutting the ropes. However, they realized that to do this would be dangerous because one flap of Dora's tail could kill a rescuer.

At last 25 people were involved in the rescue, each with a defined task. Some were in the rescue boats and some were on land, including veterinarians and dispatchers. Someone commented that sometimes it takes a village to save one animal or one person, but it's worth it.

The rescuers had such compassion for the trapped whale that they decided to take the risk and attempt to free her. Diving into the water, they cut one line after another, hoping that the whale would not panic and fight them before they got the job done. Fortunately, Dora floated passively in the water the whole time. It was as if she knew the rescuers didn't want to harm her. Finally the last line was cut and she was freed from the entanglement.

Once she was free, rather than swim toward the open sea, Dora swam in what the rescuers described as circles of joy. It was as if she wanted to rejoice after being given this unexpected gift of love. After her joyful swim of celebration, she came back to each diver, one at a time, and gently nudged him, as though to say, "Thank you." The rescuers were touched by the whale's human-like response. It was one of the most moving experiences they ever had.

What a wonderful story. Like the whale, our lives can sometimes become so entangled with struggles and problems that we can hardly stay afloat. But what a comfort it is to have others come to our rescue, to be there for us, willing to help free us from the strings that bind us. And, as the humpback whale taught us, showing gratitude to those who help us can make a difference in their lives as well.

REFLECTION

1. Whales don't sing because they have an answer. They sing because they have a song. Everyone has a song. It's a good reason to sing.
2. Grateful rescued people help to rescue others. Gratefulness is empowering.
3. *Give thanks in all circumstances.* —I Thessalonians 5:18

SUBSTITUTE THE WORD "TODAY" FOR "SOMEDAY"

How fast the todays become yesterdays.

There's a story about a woman whose favorite word was "SOMEDAY." She was often heard expressing the following thoughts:

"There are some things I want to do Someday. There are so many things I want to say Someday. There are so many people I want to hug and say 'I love you,' and perhaps I will Someday. All the trials and hurts and disappointments I've endured in my life will somehow have meaning for me Someday. When I have the time, I'll sit and reminisce about all the people and events and special moments that have meant so much to me over the years. I'll smile and cry and long to relive each special moment one more time. Someday."

Someday never came for the lady. But the end of her life did. Her tombstone read:

"Too many Somedays. Not enough Todays."

Dreams and goals and achievements never happen when you use "Someday." You can make them happen only when you work on them "Today." You will experience a sense of excitement when you start working on a goal. Your adrenalin starts flowing. You see possibilities. You have purpose. Your life has meaning. It feels so good to get things done "Today."

The following poem reminds us what happens when we use Someday instead of Today.

Someday I'll do the things I promised to do.
I'll read that poem you wanted me to.
Someday I'll take the time for coffee,
and we'll sit and talk, just you and me.

We'll get out that game you like to play.
I'll do it Someday but not today.
I got so used to saying Someday
that somehow life just slipped away.
The Somedays are now the Yesterdays.
If only I could relive those Todays.
I'll make it up to you some way.
I promise I'll do it. Someday.

All the things we hope to do someday cannot be done yesterday. Today is all we have. It takes a bit of creative thinking to figure out all that it takes to get started and more creative thinking to make the dream a reality.

REFLECTION

1. The road that's called Someday takes you to a place called Nowhere. —Tony Robbins
2. Someday is not a day of the week. It's not on the calendar. It doesn't exist.
3. *Do not boast about tomorrow, for you do not know what a day may bring forth.* — Proverbs 27:1

WHERE TO FND THE BEST TREASURE OF ALL

Memories are timeless treasures of the heart.

When I was a child, my cousins would come and we would often play a game called "'Who can find the treasure?" We would take an empty tin can from the kitchen and stuff a small toy in it. Then one person would hide the treasure. Once it was hidden, the others would search for it. The person who hid the treasure had to tell the others, as they searched, if they were hot (getting close to the treasure) or cold (getting far away).

Everyone loved the game. It was a thrill to be the one who found the hidden treasure. In our young minds, it wasn't an old tin can stuffed with a worn out toy at all. It was a treasure worth a large fortune.

Maybe there's something within all of us that makes us want to find a treasure. Maybe that's why the state lotteries and those scratch-off cards are so popular. We fantasize about getting rich quick.

A few years ago, a friend of mine, who was a law enforcement officer, took me through monitored locked doors to observe the room where the Florida Lottery was conducted. He showed me all the counterfeit tickets people had created in an effort to win the lottery. Many of the tickets looked amazingly authentic. Then he showed me the room that housed the machine that popped out those little balls with numbers on them. The machine was behind heavy glass so armed guards could watch the process.

I was impressed with the tight security but couldn't help but wonder how our priorities got so distorted. How did we go from an old tin can to a tightly secured room that produced one winner out of maybe several million people searching for that elusive treasure?

It's sad "It's sad because the real treasure isn't in a tin can or a lottery ticket. It isn't in a "thing" at all. The best treasure of all can be found in the mirror. Look closely at the image you see. Look deeply. The real treasure is within you. You don't have to search further. Open the treasure chest of potential that lies within you. What's there sparkles with value and worth. You are rich with possibilities. It's there for you to explore and enjoy. Don't keep your treasure hidden. In the cemeteries is buried an enormous treasure of untapped potential, people who never realized their worth. Don't be one of them. Dig into your potential and use it.

REFLECTION

1. Hidden deep within you is a treasure of blessings, waiting to be discovered. May you take the time to discover what is your unique treasure. It's there waiting to be opened. Don't let it go undiscovered.
2. "Your life is a treasure and you are so much more than you know." —Robert Bach.
3. *For where your treasure is, there your heart will be also.* —Matthew 6:21

YOUR LIFE CAN BE MENDED

For when I am weak, then I am strong.
— 2 Corinthians 12:10

I grew up in the '50s, those nostalgic "happy days." Eight sisters and brothers and two parents lived on a little farm in rural Ohio, with dogs, cats, chickens, cows, and pigs. We lived in a one room school house that had been converted into a home. What fond memories I have of those years. They are etched in my heart forever.

We had nothing, yet we had everything. We had little entertainment, yet we were entertained. In our little nearby town, we had free outdoor movies projected onto a sheet fastened between two poles. We had ice cream socials, fish fries, hayrides, and hotdogs roasted over a blazing bonfire.

We were joined by friends and relatives who lived nearby, and our times together were rich and full. We sat and talked and laughed a lot and sometimes cried. We had love and togetherness that's still somewhere inside me.

We didn't have money to buy many things, so we had to mend and repair what became damaged and broken, maybe repair something several times before it wore out. Nothing was ever wasted.

We kept things because they had worth. We mended things because they had value. But there comes a time when there can be no more fixing. Things completely wear out, and you have to let go of them.

This is true of humans as well. All lives have value, and, like the things we treasure, they get damaged or start to wear out and need mending.

My mother and father both died in the hospital. In the loneliness of their hospital rooms I recalled that they had been mended and repaired many times, and it was painful to know that they had reached a point where they could be mended no more. They were completely worn out. I had to let them go.

There comes a time when those we love have to leave us. But while we have them, it's important to let them know we value them, that we love them, and that we will be there for them as much as possible to help them mend when they get damaged and need repair.

Sometimes it means mending our relationship with them and repairing any strains that have occurred, fixing cracks, and restoring torn pieces. It's important to not let any time be wasted. It's crucial to make the moments count. This, of course, is true of all relationships.

Relationships that have been mended bring healing, and with healing comes well-being. Restored relationships get rid of raw edges and bring about a peace of mind. Reconciliation often makes things better than they were before.

The older we get the more important it is to mend relationships. We're working on limited time. We need to free ourselves from as many conflicts and struggles as we can so we can experience the best quality of life possible.

That's the creative element in all of this. It's creative to think about how to mend and repair our relationships. Each one may require a different approach, a different twist, but for each one we mend, the greater our well-being will be.

Kintsugi is the wonderful centuries-old Japanese art of fixing broken objects with a special lacquer dusted with powdered gold. It actually adds value to the broken object. It's based on the idea that in embracing flaws and imperfections, instead of hiding or disguising them, you can create an even stronger, more beautiful piece of art.

Every break in an object is unique and instead of repairing an item to make it look new, the technique actually highlights the "scars." In the process of repairing objects that have been cracked or broken, something more unique, beautiful, and resilient is created....even more beautiful than the original.

What a beautiful metaphor. All lives can be mended. If there's something in your life that needs mending, be creative and touch it up with lacquer and powdered gold. Do whatever it takes to fix it and make it better than new. But don't try to hide the scar. The scar is a reminder that you are human and you have overcome. Be comforted to know that mended lives are often stronger and more beautiful than before.

REFLECTION

1. Relationships that get broken but then mended are often stronger than before.
2. Individuals who have been broken are often those who can best help others mend.
3. God can restore what is broken and change it into something amazing. *In all your ways acknowledge him, and he will make your paths straight.* —Proverbs 3:6

ACCOMPLISH YOUR GOALS A FEW MINUTES AT A TIME

Dreams are best achieved one step at a time.

Author and educator John Erskine was fourteen when he learned a valuable lesson about life. His piano teacher asked him, "John, how many times a week do you practice and for how long?"

John replied that he tried to practice for an hour each day.

His teacher said, "Well, don't do that. When you grow up, time won't come in long stretches. Practice in minutes whenever you can find time, before school, after lunch, after school, between chores. Spread your practice throughout the day and music will become part of your life."

John followed the teacher's advice and became a concert pianist. He later served as president of the Juilliard School of Music and director of the Metropolitan Opera Association.

John also applied the teacher's advice to his writing interests. He loved to write, but he had a busy schedule, so he wrote in five and ten minute snatches. To his astonishment, he finished a manuscript in one week. In addition to music, writing became a part of his life, and he ended up writing over 45 books.

One of the reasons I love oil painting is because I can paint in snatches of time. Unlike acrylic paints, oil paints do not dry quickly. I can paint for 15 or twenty 20 minutes, go work on other tasks, then go back later and paint some more, sometimes even the next day. Sometimes I wake up in the middle of the night, paint for a while, then go back to bed (I don't necessarily advise this, but it works for me.). When I did my first art show in June, 2018, I painted in snatches of time and was able to complete 120 paintings in one year

Dreams rarely come in large chunks of time. So, whatever your dreams are, you can make them happen by seizing bits and pieces of time as you can, a few minutes here, a few minutes there, a half hour here, a half hour there. Before you know it, you will have accomplished your goal.

Like *The Little Engine That Could*, tell yourself, "I think I can, I think I can, I think I can."

REFLECTION

1. Time is a precious gift. Cherish it and use it wisely because there's a limit to how much of it you will be blessed to have in life.
2. It's not about "having time" to do things. It's about "making time" to do what matters to you. There's a difference and you get to choose.
3. *There is a time for everything, and a season for every activity under the heavens.* — Ecclesiastes 3:1

THE FIVE-FOLD
PHILOSOPHY OF THE ANT

One of earth's smallest creatures can teach
some of life's biggest lessons.

D id you ever try to destroy an ant hill? It's almost impossible. If you
pour some kind of anti-ant granules on the hill, the ants just pack
their bags, move to another location, and build a new home.

I see ants in my backyard almost every day. You might say I've befriended
them. They're fascinating creatures. I've learned a lot about life by studying them.
Their five-fold philosophy of work is a great example of how we should function as
human beings. From my point of view, here's how their philosophy can be applied:

- Carry your share of the work. Every ant works, no exceptions. Each
  one knows what to do and does it. No shirking of duty.
- Know where you're going. Every day ants have purpose. They know
  where they need to go. They accomplish something every day.
- Stay positive and never give up. When things go wrong, they keep going.
  If obstacles get in their way, they either remove them or go around them
  or go over them. If their home gets destroyed, they rebuild.
- Work as a team. Ants support the common goal of the group. They
  do what's needed to maintain the group effort. Each one knows its
  function in the group and does it.
- Love where you live. Ants are dedicated to their home. They keep
  their home neat and maintained. If damage occurs, they repair it
  immediately.

Ants are amazing creatures. Major corporations have studied their work ethics, their accounting, and their self-control. They have also studied their means of communication and farming techniques.

Most fascinating to me are the studies that have been done on the ant's creativity. An example of this is how an ant solves the problem of a deep ravine. It finds a stick and uses it as a bridge to get across the ravine. The resourcefulness of the ant is mind-boggling.

What great examples ants are. Their five-fold philosophy is a model of ingenuity that, when applied, leads to successful living for humans.

Without realizing they were doing it, the Wright brothers applied the five-fold philosophy of the ant to help them create one of the greatest inventions the world has ever received: the airplane.

The Wright brothers each shared the workload in working on their airplane. They knew where they were going and what they wanted to accomplish. They stayed positive and never gave up, even in the face of constant ridicule. They worked as a team and each knew what he needed to do to get the job done.

In a sense, their workshop was their home and they loved being there, spending hours and hours to achieve their dream. They also ultimately built a home in their later years, built to their specifications. Home was important to them. Henry Ford acquired the Wright brothers' home in 1937 and relocated it from Dayton, Ohio, to Dearborn, Michigan, and placed it in the Greenfield Village museum complex, where it is preserved for visitors to view.

Nature is, indeed, the world's greatest classroom.

REFLECTION

1. To have purpose in life is to ache deep within your soul for what you want to achieve, to dream of obtaining that which your heart longs to grasp,

2. Successful people are not the ones who never fail; they're the ones who never give up.

3. *Go to the ant....consider its ways and be wise! It has no commander, no overseer or ruler, yet it stores its provisions in summer and gathers its food at harvest.* (Proverbs 6:6-8)

MAY YOU BE BLESSED WITH AN ANAM CARA (SOUL MATE)

Once you find your soul mate, never let go.

Anam Cara is a beautiful ancient Celtic phrase which loosely translates as "soul mate." *Anam* is the Irish Gaelic word for "soul." *Cara* is the Irish Gaelic word for "friend." Thus, the literal meaning is "soul friend.

Anam Cara is a special relationship between two people, such as spouse, lover, friend, family member, teacher, or spiritual guide. It's a Celtic philosophy and Irish belief that two souls with this unique connection are stronger together than they are apart. It's similar to King Solomon's wise philosophy that states, "Two are better than one, because they have a good return for their labor. If either of them falls down, one can help the other up."

An *Anam Cara* is the soul mate with whom you can share your deepest hopes and dreams and the intimacies of your life. When you are blessed with *Anam Cara,* you have arrived at a most sacred place, a sense of belonging, a sense of home. It is with your *Anam Cara* that your life feels complete.

The Celtic ideal is for every person to be blessed with this beautiful relationship. I learned about the concept of *Anam Cara* from a friend with whom I was having coffee one morning. This was new to me, and I was so intrigued by it that I went home and researched more information about it. I personally love to discover new things, and what I discovered was enlightening to me and gave me new insights into relationships.

After doing my research, I got another cup of coffee, went outside, and sat down on the bench in my meditation garden. It's quiet and peaceful there and conducive to reflection and meditation.

I thought a lot about *Anam Cara* and how special and meaningful it is for a person to have a soul mate. Such a relationship is perhaps a once-in-a-lifetime thing. It's a person you never get tired of being with. You can talk for hours and never get bored. You can share anything and not be judged. This is the one person who is in touch with your soul and encourages you to explore the exciting world of self-discovery. It feels like this person is the other half of you and makes your life complete. You both feel a powerful, indescribable force that only the two of you can feel.

As they say, once you have found your soul mate, never let that person go. If you have such a relationship and then lose it, through death or other reasons, you have experienced perhaps the most beautiful relationship possible, and you can savor the memory of it the rest of your life.

And perhaps it should be said that it's never too late to find an *Anam Cara* soul mate. Age has nothing to do with how intense or beautiful the relationship is going to be. The key is to find that one person with whom your soul connects even if it is for a short time. Having an *Anam Cara* relationship, even for a short time, is like an eternity of joy.

The whole concept of *Anam Cara* digs deeply into creativity. It requires creative thinking to sort out what you might want and look for in a soul mate, especially since it's typically a once-in-a-lifetime occurrence.

REFLECTION

1. Though you may experience love many times in your lifetime, only one will burn your soul forever.
2. Two souls that are meant to be together somehow know about each other and are willing to search forever until they meet.
3. *Two are better than one, because they have a good return for their work; if either of them falls down, one can help the other up.* — Ecclesiastes 4:9-10

APPLYING COLLEGE FOOTBALL'S TARGETING RULE TO CONVERSATION

Speak wisely, because once spoken, hurtful words cannot be retracted.

College football has a rule called "targeting." It's when one player tackles another and his helmet comes in contact with the helmet of the player he is tackling, causing harm or potential harm. When this happens, the referee throws the yellow flag, and the player who did the targeting is ejected from the game.

Wouldn't it be interesting if we passed a law that said, "If you use hurtful words directed at another person, causing that person emotional pain, a yellow flag will be thrown and you will be called for 'targeting' and will have to leave the conversation."

Come to think of it, we already have a rule that deals with this issue. It's called *The Golden Rule:* "Do to others what you would want them to do to you." In reference to conversation, we might reframe it to say, "'Say to others what you would want them to say to you."

In football, no one wants to get hit in the head by someone else's hard helmet. It hurts and it's dangerous. Players have been carried off the field after being targeted. The rule doesn't keep "targeting" from happening, but it has reduced how often it happens. It also directly addresses the guilty player and makes him realize that what he did was wrong.

It's the same with communication. No one likes to be hit with words from another person that are painful and can cause emotional distress.

The Golden Rule says if you don't like being hurt by words directed at you by another person, then don't do it to others. Don't use words that "target" others and cause them pain.

What's interesting is that everyone can carry a symbolic "yellow flag" with them when having a conversation. Then, when someone causes you pain by hitting you with hurtful words, you can throw the "yellow flag" by saying, "What you're saying is painful to me. Your words hurt. I don't want to hear any more of them. If you continue to use them, I'm either going to leave the conversation or ask you to leave."

The Golden Rule has stood the test of time. It still works.

The creative part about this is to think about the words you use and how you use them. For example, examine whether or not you are guilty of "targeting." By doing so, you will learn to make better word choices in your conversations. You can also recall how it felt when you were "targeted" with hurtful words.

Never allow yourself to say words that are so painful to another person that the individual has to be carried off the field of conversation. That person may never forget the hurtful words you spoke. It is not unusual for people to remember painful words years later.

The tongue is one part of the body that has no bone structure, yet it is strong enough to break a person's heart. There's an old saying that reminds people to taste their words before they spit them out. There's much wisdom in that saying.

REFLECTION

1. Words have power and sometimes can be explosive. Handle with care.
2. Verbal abuse often does more damage than physical abuse.
3. *Let your conversation be always full of grace, seasoned with salt.* — *Colossians 4:6*

MY DAD, THE ENIGMA

No one teaches dads how to be a dad,
they just somehow do their best.

I wish my dad had permitted me to know him better. He was such an enigma to me. I always sensed there were so many interesting things about his life he could have shared but simply chose not to. I would loved to have heard little anecdotes about his life as he was growing up, like what kind of games he played, what he and his friends did for entertainment, who his close friends were, what his family talked about at the dinner table, what kind of books he liked to read, or what it was like attending a one room school. If only I had asked questions like these while he was still alive, maybe he would have answered them.....if only.

I do know some basic facts about his life. I know he was born in 1901, grew up on his parents' farm in rural Ohio, and was the second of four children. I also know he had horses because I saw old photos of him with his horses. In every photo he had a smile on his face. But what I wish I knew were the little things — like what he named his horses, where he went when he rode them, how much they meant to him, things that would have given me glimpses into what he was like as a teenager.

I know my dad's first car was a Model T Ford. I know my mother and a few of her friends stopped to admire the car when he was in town (and maybe admire my dad) and that's how my parents met. I know that story because my mother shared it, not my dad. He never shared what attracted him to my mother other than the fact that he once jokingly said she knew nothing about farming or how to cook an egg. But in a way I guess that appealed to him because he decided to marry her and raise a large family of eight children (I was number seven).

My parents got married as The Great Depression was making its presence known. Times were hard and my dad regularly worked two jobs to support his growing family. He was foremost a farmer and he worked hard at it and I sensed that being in the fields, planting crops, cultivating, and harvesting them afforded him a certain solitude that he enjoyed. His tanned face and arms conveyed the fact that he was constantly in the sun. Though we children never commented on it to him, we often chuckled at his "farmer's tan," which was arms tanned up only to the elbows, the result of rolled up sleeves. He never wore short sleeved shirts or tee shirts. Instead, he wore what we called his dark green "uniform" shirts with long sleeves year round. He never shared why he preferred to wear these types of clothes every day. He just did.

My dad's part-time jobs while farming full-time were at the local stone quarry and the nearby hay mill, both requiring hard labor. I recall seeing him come home after a long day of working two jobs, tired and dirty, sit in his favorite chair, and fall asleep while reading the newspaper. But not once did I hear him complain about working two jobs. He eventually took a full-time job working for the Ohio Department of Highways while still maintaining his farm work. It wasn't until I was an adult that I was able to fully grasp how devoted he was to his family and how willing he was to do what he needed to do to support them.

I don't recall that my dad ever played childhood games with us children, that he took us fishing or threw the ball with us, or that he ever held us on his lap and read stories to us. I don't recall that he ever attended a parent-teacher conference or attended school functions, or that he took us to Sunday school. I don't think he was inclined to take part in family recreational activities, but even if he would have wanted to I doubt that after working two jobs each day he had much energy left over to participate.

The older I get the more I admire him for the tremendous commitment he had to his family. I wish I had seen this more clearly at the time and let him know how much I appreciated his efforts.

My grandmother died when I was seven years old and my dad had concerns about my grandfather living alone. So he made arrangements for us to move in with my grandfather on his farm and care for him. Up to this point I had not known my grandfather well, but over the next few years became aware of how much alike he and my father were. It was amazing how similar their values, interests, and behaviors were.

When I was sixteen, my grandfather had a stroke and was hospitalized. He was incoherent and at times combative with the hospital staff. My father said little about it but I could sense how sad he was about my grandfather's condition. He faithfully visited him in the morning before he went to work and later before he went home from work.

On one occasion my dad asked me if I wanted to go with him to the hospital. I was surprised at the invitation and gladly agreed to accompany him. What I experienced at that visit gave me insights into my dad that I will never forget and opened my eyes to a whole different side of him.

I watched as dad took his electric shaver and shaved my grandfather. I was amazed at how careful and gentle he was. I watched as he ran his hands over his father's face and rubbed his forehead with a tenderness I had never seen in him. And I watched as he examined the restraints that were on my grandfather's arms because of his combativeness and I saw tears well in my dad's eyes. I watched this man that I didn't know very well hover over his father with a compassion I didn't think existed. That visit was a moment in time that froze in my mind forever. I'll never forget it. He said nothing about the visit after we left but what I saw was worth a thousand words.

A second moment in time is frozen in my mind. My dad, who never attended school functions, showed up at my high school graduation. He never told me he was going to be there and I didn't expect it. He just showed up. He had on the only suit he owned, the suit he only wore for special occasions, mostly funerals, and his shoes were dusted off and shined. It was all I could do to keep from crying as I looked out at the audience and saw him sitting there with my mother. As usual, he didn't talk about it after the ceremony. He didn't slap me on the back and say, "Congratulations, son, I'm proud of you." He didn't have to. He was just there. Again, what I saw was worth a thousand words.

A third moment in time that's frozen in my mind was when my eight year old niece died from leukemia. I'm not sure how it happened that my dad was riding in the car with me as we left the cemetery. What I do remember is him crying and saying, "I wish the Lord would have taken me instead of her." I honestly think he would have given his life for hers.

Dad died when I was forty-one. I miss him. I wish I could have had more years with him. I wish I could re-live pieces of the past and share stories with him. I wish I could have a cup of coffee with him or maybe lots of coffee (he loved his coffee) and just talk. I wish we could have hugged each other and said, "I love you."

As I look back over those forty-one years I had with him, much of his life is still an enigma to me. There's so much I don't know. But what I do know is that I have been fortunate to have had some important glimpses of him as a dad and as a person. And the glimpses have shown me how special he was. I didn't realize it at the time, but he shared much more of his life than I thought. What he shared is enough. I'm convinced he thoroughly enjoyed his role as a "dad," but he did it his way. I'm just glad he was my dad.

But I wish I would have asked him more questions.

For some reason, writing this was both enlightening and healing. I highly recommend that you examine your close relationships, choose one of them and take the time to write about how you view this person. Be honest and objective. Write what you know. And when you do, look for the positives as well as the negatives. If needed, do a little research to discover as much as possible about this person. It was a healing process for me and I think I would be the same for you.

REFLECTION

1. The best gift my dad ever gave me: he believed in me.
2. There's comfort beyond words when you feel your dad protecting you.
3. *A righteous man leads a blameless life; blessed are his children after him.*
   — Proverbs 20:7

A HUG IS WORTH MORE THAN A THOUSAND WORDS

There's something about a hug that says,
"Everything's going to be okay."

Someone once said that a hug was invented to let people know you love them without saying a word. I believe that's true because one good hug says so much and is so meaningful. No words are necessary. A good silent hug says it all.

When people talk about the importance of good communication, they often forget to mention hugging. Hugging is perhaps the most beautiful form of communication there is because it lets the other person know they matter. It expresses love, warmth, and caring. And it cuts across all language barriers. Never underestimate the power of a hug.

Sometimes when you really need a hug and someone comes and hugs you tight, you just don't want to let go. It feels so good and means so much. A summary of some of the research on hugging gives insights into why hugging is so important. If you're like me, you'll be both fascinated and surprised with what the research says.

1. Hugs release four happy neurotransmitters: oxytocin, dopamine, serotonin, and endorphins.
2. Oxytocin - It is often referred to as the "cuddle" hormone because it creates intimacy and trust and builds healthy relationships. When we hug, it is released into our bodies by our pituitary gland, lowering our

cortisol levels, the hormone responsible for stress, high blood pressure, and heart disease.

3. Dopamine - It is responsible for giving us that feel-good feeling. It is often referred to as the "pleasure" hormone. Procrastination, self-doubt, and lack of enthusiasm are linked to low levels of dopamine. Hugs are said to adjust those levels.

4. Serotonin - It is responsible for elevating mood. It creates happiness and helps reduce depression.

5. Endorphin - It is responsible for causing pleasure, and negating pain and sadness. Even the cuddling of pets has a soothing effect that reduces stress levels.

6. A really good sincere hug will increase your sense of bonding and belonging, increase your sense of pleasure, make you feel good and confident, and decrease stress.

7. Research also shows that hugging is effective at healing sickness, disease, loneliness, depression, anxiety, and stress.

8. Hugging builds trust and a sense of safety.

What's creative about a hug? Well, it's creative to think about what a hug means to you, how it makes you feel, and what effect it has on you. It's creative to think about the different kinds of hugs that people give you. Which kind do you like best? What do hugs tell you about the other person? What does your response to the hugs tell you about yourself?

I'm a hugger. I believe hugging is a natural way to greet someone you know or to say goodbye to them. I also believe the research that says hugging can be healing.

One day when I was walking across our campus in the retirement community where I live, I met a lady I had known for a long time. She did not look well. She told me she had just gotten out of the hospital and felt worn out. She shared that she was also dealing with some frustrations. I said, "Do you need a hug?" She responded, "Oh, yes. I sure do." So I hugged her and she thanked me. I believe it was a healing hug that was given right when she needed some support and encouragement. That's what hugs do.

I notice that men often have difficulty hugging another man, especially if they've been raised in the United States. Somehow men have been made to believe that it's not masculine to hug. Yet in many countries, men hug each other as part of a greeting. It's just a natural thing to do.

It's sad that we let society determine whom we can hug and whom we cannot. In my opinion, a handshake is not a good substitute for a hug. It's also sad that men miss out on some of the benefits of hugging.

My father-in-law was not one to hug another man. For years we simply shook hands as part of our greeting. One day when he was older, and so was I, I greeted him with the usual handshake but then surprised him with a hug. The look on his face was priceless. But he said nothing. He seemed okay with it.

Thereafter, when we greeted each other or said goodbye, we hugged. It became an okay thing to do. I give him a lot of credit for being receptive to a hug from me. He was raised in a Ukrainian home where hugging another man evidently was not part of a greeting. Once he and I started hugging as part of our greeting, a cultural tradition was broken. I'm glad I took the initiative to give him that first hug because it seemed to change our relationship. An invisible barrier was finally removed and it allowed us to bond. That's what hugs do.

REFLECTION

1. Hugs are silent, but they speak volumes.
2. The most comforting place you can be is inside a hug.
3. *He ran to meet him and embraced him, and fell on his neck and kissed him, and they wept.* — Genesis 33.4

GIVE YOURSELF CREDIT
FOR EFFORT

There's honor in trying your best, even if you don't succeed.

Did you ever notice that there's a tendency to always define success based on achievement?

You're a success only if you accomplish your goal. You're a success if you come in first. You're a success if you win the blue ribbon. You're a success if you win the competition. People focus only on the end result, the "finished product." But is that all there really is to success?

Putting a man on the moon was a tremendous accomplishment, but what about all the years of effort it took to get him there? What do you know about the individuals who were behind the scenes?

Sitting down in someone's home and enjoying a wonderful meal results in compliments about the food, but what about all the planning, shopping, cooking, and presentation it took to get it on the table?

The runner who wins a marathon race gets praise and awards for finishing first, but what about all the training it took to run the race, and what about the effort put forth by the many others who also finished the race behind the winner?

Thomas Edison once said, "Great accomplishments depend not so much on ingenuity as on hard work. Genius is one percent inspiration and ninety-nine percent perspiration."

Many people refuse to even try to accomplish certain things because they think it's going to be too hard or they're afraid they will try and fail. Perhaps it's time to start giving credit, or praise, or compliments, for people's efforts, even if they didn't achieve their goal.

This is particularly applicable for older adults. It's often harder for them to accomplish the things they used to do. As a result, it's often easier for them to not even try. They don't feel good about trying and failing. Yet, if they focused on their effort, the fact that they tried, and gave themselves credit for making the attempt, they would feel better about themselves.

Effort itself can be a goal. It's a goal if we say, "I'm going to give it my best effort. I'll try my best." Then, if you do indeed try your best, you can feel good about accomplishing your goal.

Not everyone can win the competition. Not everyone can finish the marathon. But everyone can try. We need to give more credit to those who try their best regardless of the outcome.

This was all made clear to me when I was in elementary school. For some reason, spelling came easy to me. We had weekly spelling tests and I rarely had to study very much for the tests. I usually got all the words correct and as a result received an A on my paper and also a gold star. There was a boy in the class who struggled with spelling. He studied hard for the tests. His mother would help him study and drill him over and over on each word. However, when it came time for the tests, he would always misspell some of the words. As a result he often received a C or a D from the teacher and never received a gold star.

I felt sorry for him. He tried his best but still got a C or a D. He received no credit or praise for his effort. It doesn't seem fair.

In my opinion, I think it's time we acknowledge effort in the same way we acknowledge achievement.

REFLECTION

1. One of the things you have to prepare for in life is not getting credit for effort. But that's something you can do for yourself.
2. You have achieved success if you have tried hard and improved — you're better today than you were yesterday.
3. *Let us therefore make every effort to do what leads to peace and to mutual edification.* —Romans 14:19

HOW TO HAVE A BLUE-RIBBON RELATIONSHIP

Take the time to know what you want in
a relationship, then nurture it.

O ver the years as I counseled and worked with individuals, I had
the opportunity to see relationships from every angle, up close and
personal, inside and out. I've seen what worked and what didn't. I've
seen pain and conflict in relationships and I've seen healing and joy. I've seen
individuals give up and separate and I've seen them forgive and reconcile. In
50 years of work, I've pretty much seen it all. Fortunately, much of it has been
a positive experience.

Of course all relationships are not the same. Each relationship has its own
set of unique circumstances. And whether it's a relationship involving siblings,
friends, married couples, parent and child, or grandparent and grandchild,
both individuals in a relationship have to work on it. Effective relationships
don't just happen. As my wife of 62 years will say, "It takes two to tango," or
as my grandfather used to say, "It takes two flints to make a fire."

Listed below are four key words I consider to be characteristic of a blue-
ribbon relationship. I have found that they are the qualities that make a
relationship work. I believe these four words serve as good reminders of what
to look for and nurture in a relationship.

LOVE
Anyone can say, "I love you." But saying it isn't enough. Active
love shows the other person on a regular basis that you love

her/him. Effective love is unconditional. It involves loving a person without putting conditions on the relationship, loving the other person in spite of his/her mistakes and flaws. This holds true for all relationships. Sometimes individuals assume that loving someone is the sole reason to be in a relationship, and it's the only thing they focus on. They forget about or ignore all the other important ingredients. This is often the reason that relationships fail or go stale. Love is the foundation for sure, but other qualities have to be included and worked on as well.

COMMUNICATION

There's effective communication, poor communication, and no communication. By your actions, you demonstrate which one you practice. There's a difference between meaningful communication and just talking. Talking is simply expressing words, not necessarily with any feeling. Communication involves being transparent, sharing your thoughts, feelings, hopes, dreams, wants, needs, hurts, and frustrations. It involves being able to disagree without having to be right, without blaming, without demanding or threatening. It involves compromise, being able to say, "I'm sorry," or "I forgive you." Words have power and can be used constructively to help, encourage, inspire, even heal, or they can be used destructively to criticize, hurt, harm, and humiliate. Always choose your words wisely and constantly examine what kind of words you are using.

TIME

The best way to kill a relationship is to neglect it. The only way to develop and maintain a relationship is to spend time on it. You have to water flowers to keep them blooming, and you have to nurture a relationship to keep it alive and growing. It means taking the time to do things together, making it a priority to set aside regular time for the other person. It means willingly participating in the interests of the other person, sharing in their hopes and dreams. It means taking the time to understand each other's needs and wants.

FAITH

Faith and relationships go hand in hand. Faith gives couples the strength to overcome challenges and obstacles that could harm their relationship. It's the glue that keeps them together during their most difficult times. Having spiritual intimacy and compassionate love for each other makes the relationship strong. Having faith in each other to always be there whenever needed guides them through their best times and their worst times.

It's important to note that sometimes relationships become broken. Two individuals decide to end their relationship and separate. Hopefully they will both find healing.

I encourage you to sit down and make a list of the qualities you want in your relationships. It's healthy to identify what's important to you. Think about the words that would strengthen your relationships and make them work. Think of creative ways you can express and nurture each quality.

REFLECTION

1. It takes two to build a relationship; it takes two to improve a relationship.
2. It takes two to keep a relationship alive and well.
3. *Above all, love each other deeply.* — I Peter 4:8

BEAUTY IS LIKE A BUTTERFLY

Others can see your beauty even when you cannot.

One of my favorite stories is about a little first grade student named Allie and her art teacher. The story has been passed on to me so I don't know Allie or the teacher personally. I just know that the story tugs at my heart.

Allie went to her art teacher in tears. "Why are you crying?" the teacher asked.

Allie held up a blank sheet of paper and said, "My daddy said I was beautiful and I wanted to draw it. But I don't know what beautiful looks like."

The art teacher picked Allie up, put her on her lap and said, "That's a very profound question, young lady. Let me see if I can answer it. Have you ever seen a butterfly?"

Allie shook her head yes.

"Well," said the teacher, "people look at butterflies and see all the different colors and all the different patterns in their wings, and they say how beautiful they are. But did you know that butterflies can's see their own wings? They can't see how beautiful they are, but everyone else can. You are like the butterfly, Allie. You might not be able to see your own beauty, but your daddy can. He can see your patterns and colors. The patterns he sees in you are your behaviors, how you act, how you treat others, the kindness you show. The colors he sees in you are like a box of crayons that you keep in your heart. Beauty is within you. It's how you use your crayons to color the world with your love and brighten the lives of others. So perhaps you can draw a butterfly on your paper and see beauty in the patterns and colors. Would you like to do that?"

Allie smiled and shook her head yes. She took her paper and went to her desk, relieved that she now knew how she was going to draw "beautiful."

What an interesting story. And what a profound message.

Another story about beauty that I like is the one about the little rose that struggled to survive in a neglected garden surrounded by weeds. The rose felt lonely and sad as its petals began to fade.

"I have nothing to offer," the rose thought. "I am hidden among these weeds. My petals are no longer bright and crisp with color, and my fragrance is weak."

One day a group of ladies was taking a tour of the gardens in the old estate that was now for sale. One of the ladies noticed the rose and said, "Look at that poor rose amidst those weeds. It must have been quite beautiful in its day. What a pity its days are over."

The estate's gardener was standing nearby and heard the lady's comments. The gardener was old and overwhelmed with trying to keep the gardens free of weeds and beautiful. He had forgotten about the rose that was planted amidst the weeds.

The gardener went to the rose, leaned down and sniffed. "You still have a little fragrance," he said. 'Let me get you away from these weeds and take you inside."

The gardener cut the rose, took it inside the old home, got a beautiful bud vase, filled it with fresh water, and placed the rose in it. "There," he said. "Perhaps you will feel better." He sat the vase down on a small antique table in front of an ornate mirror, and left.

The group of ladies who toured the gardens were now touring the home. The lady who had seen the rose amidst the weeds and pitied it, noticed the rose on the table in front of the mirror.

"Oh, my, look at that beautiful rose," she said. She leaned down and gently sniffed. "What a sweet, old-fashioned fragrance," she said. "I simply must have the rose bush from which it came. When they have the estate sale I will buy it, no matter how much it costs. I'm sure it will be expensive."

After the ladies left, the rose looked at its image in the mirror. "I can't believe how nice I look," she thought. "Getting away from the weeds and having a little water makes a difference. My petals have come alive. And my fragrance is still sweet. I feel like I have been reborn."

Like the rose, every person has a fragrance. How you live your life is your aroma. Your petals may be vibrant and beautiful, but it's your aroma that draws people to you. It's your aroma that people remember long after your petals fade. So live your life in such a way that your aroma transcends your presence and touches many lives.

REFLECTION

1. Yes, you are imperfect and flawed, but that's what makes you so appealing, so unique, so beautiful.
2. Always remember, the people who have the courage to be their own authentic self are the beautiful people.
3. *He has made everything beautiful in its time.* —Ecclesiastes 3:11

A LITTLE GIRL'S GIFT OF LOVE

The greatest gift of all is love.

Our family Christmas in 1968 is one I'll never forget. Our six-year-old daughter Claudia gave me a gift that tugged at my heart and taught me something about love that only a child can teach.

Our four children usually did their Christmas shopping at the elementary school's Secret Santa Shop. Items were donated by community members throughout the year and just before Christmas children could pick out items to purchase that were reasonably priced, ranging from a quarter to a dollar. Since my wife and I and our four children survived on my rather meager teacher's salary, the Secret Santa Shop was an ideal place for our children to buy their Christmas gifts.

We gave each child enough money to buy small items for family members and it was up to them to budget their money so they would be able to get something for each person. We thought this was a good way for them to learn to manage their money but also to experience the joy of giving to others. We were always amazed at how well they did and how personal their gifts were.

Our daughter Claudia secretly told my wife that the gift she wanted to purchase for me, a handkerchief, was not in the Secret Santa Shop. She had noticed that the handkerchief I always wore in my coat pocket on Sunday morning for church was getting rather worn and she wanted to buy me a new one to replace it. She had seen on television that men's monogrammed handkerchiefs were on sale at the mall and she had her heart set on getting one with the letter C on it for me.

After daily reminders by Claudia, my wife finally worked out a time to take her to the mall to buy the handkerchief. It was just two days before Christmas.

At the mall, my wife took Claudia to the department store that advertised the handkerchiefs. They found the counter that contained the handkerchiefs and Claudia told my wife to please stand a few feet away because she wanted to do the entire transaction on her own. My wife complied but was close enough to hear Claudia's conversation with the sales clerk.

"May I help you?" the clerk asked.

"Yes, you can," Claudia said. "I want to buy one of your men's handkerchief's that comes with a letter on it.

"Good choice," the clerk said. "These handkerchiefs make wonderful gifts. We've sold a lot of them. And what letter are you looking for?"

"I would like one with a C on it," Claudia said. "My dad's name is Charles."

"Well, let me look," the clerk said. She sorted through the box of handkerchiefs once and then sorted "W a second time. "Oh, dear," she said. "We don't have any Cs left. I'm so sorry."

"Are you sure?" Claudia asked. "There must be at least one C in there. Would you please look again?"

The clerk looked again. "No, honey," she said."There are simply no Cs in the box. These handkerchiefs have been very popular this year. Is there perhaps another letter that would work?"

Claudia was silent for a moment and then said, "His last name is Lee. Do you have an L?""I sure hope so," the clerk said. She took her time and sorted through the box. She stopped and then sorted a second time. "Oh, dear," she said. "I can't seem to find an L. I just can't believe it. I'm sure I saw one in the box earlier today."

"What am I going to do?" Claudia asked. "I want to get a handkerchief for my daddy. It's very important."

"Honey, I don't know what to say," the clerk said. "Would you like for me to show you some other possibilities?"

"No, ma'am, " Claudia said. "I really want a handkerchief. My daddy needs a new one"

"I see," the clerk said. "Well, how about a plain handkerchief, one without any letters on it?"

"Oh, no," Claudia said. "I want it to be really special. With a letter on it."

"You certainly are a very determined little girl," the clerk said, "and I wish I could help you, but I simply don't have anything else to offer."

Claudia was quiet for a moment and then said, "Ma'am, just what letters do you have in that box?"

The surprised clerk said, "Well, let me see. I have some Zs and Xs, here are some Us and Vs, and here are a few Qs. Oh and here are a few Ys, Os, and Ms....."

Claudia interrupted. "Wait. I'll take the M. My daddy's middle name is Milton. That's perfect." She smiled and handed the clerk her money.

"That's a very creative solution," the clerk said. "You're one special little girl."

The clerk placed the handkerchief in a box and handed it to Claudia and also gave her back her money.

"Honey, you can keep your money," the clerk said. "That's my gift to you. I hope your daddy likes his gift. Merry Christmas."

On Christmas morning our house was filled with excitement as everyone opened their gifts. Claudia watched me closely as I opened her gift to me.

"Would you look at this," I said. "What a nice handkerchief and it's even monogrammed. Wow. And it's got an M on it for......let me guess......for Mister?"

Claudia laughed and shook her head.

"Let me guess again," I said. "An M for........Magnificent?"

Everyone laughed and Claudia again shook her head.

"Aha," I said. "I've got it. An M for.......Milton, my middle name. How thoughtful. I've never had a handkerchief for my middle name before. I bet no one on the whole wide world has ever had a handkerchief for their middle name. That makes it extra special. Thank you, Claudia. I love it."

I'm now eighty years old and I still have the handkerchief. I proudly wore it in my coat pocket for many years but it's now in a drawer for safekeeping. I get it out and look at it once in a while. And when I do, tears come to my eye because I know the tremendous love a little girl had for her daddy when she purchased it. It's amazing how one small gift, given with love, can mean so much over all these years.

Claudia now lives in New Zealand and I recently asked her if she remembered purchasing the handkerchief. "I remember it clear as a bell," she said. "I'll never forget it."

Someday the handkerchief will be passed on to Claudia. I have a note in the box that says, "This handkerchief has always been one of my most cherished gifts. There's no gift greater than the one given with love."

REFLECTION

1. To receive the gift of life is to receive the greatest gift of all.
2. I love everything about you: all that you have been, all that you are, and all that you will be. I believe great things are in store for you. — Ernest Hemingway
3. *Do everything in love* — I Corinthians 16:14

HOW A PIGEON CHANGED MY PERSPECTIVE

Things are not always what they seem.

We have two bird feeders. One is tubular with four perches. I put black oil sunflower seeds in it. The other is flat and sits atop a pole. I put a mix of seeds on it. Both feeders stand at one end of our flower bed. We can see the feeders from our sunroom. We love to sit there, work on projects, and watch the birds.

But here's the thing. I have a problem with mourning doves. And to the Audubon Society and all bird watchers out there, all I can say is, "I'm sorry, but I don't like mourning doves. And I have good reason." They come to my flat bird feeder and devour the bird seed. (They're too fat to sit on the perches of the tubular feeder like most other birds.) They just sit there in the flat feeder and eat and eat and eat. Other birds fly to the bird feeder, grab a seed or two, and fly away. Not the mourning doves. They just sit there and eat like they're ravished. And to make matters worse, they're greedy. They chase the other birds away. They want all the seed for themselves. They have no bird manners.

So what do I do? I do what I don't like to do. I go to the door, wave my arms, yell at the doves, stomp my feet, and chase them away. I say things like, "If you rascals can't share you'll have to go find food somewhere else. You can't be piggies at my bird feeder. I won't tolerate it."

And here's another thing that bugs me. Yes, I chase them away. But by the time I get back to my chair they're back. They're defiant. Or dense. Or maybe both.

We have ceiling to floor windows in our sunroom, so the doves can see me when I'm sitting in my chair. And I didn't do it intentionally, but you might say I trained those greedy seed lovers. (Smile.) After I chased them away time after time, they got the message. If they see me get up and move toward the door, they automatically fly away. I no longer have to open the door, wave insanely, and yell. But it does little good. They wait in the tree until I sit down and then they fly back to the feeder. I have to believe that Audubon Society members would understand my frustration.

One day as I was sitting in the sunroom reading a magazine, I noticed an article about a pigeon named Cher Ami. Cher Ami (which means "dear friend" in French), was one of 600 carrier pigeons used by the U.S. Army Signal Corps during World War I. Carrier pigeons were considered invaluable as a means of communication. (Remember, they didn't have iPhones.)

I learned that the average homing pigeon can fly almost 50 miles per hour. Despite their speed, they proved to be popular targets to enemy gunfire. German machine gunners were trained to spot and kill the doves with their deadly MG 08s, which were able to fire over 500 rounds per minute.

Carrier pigeons were recognized for their valiant communication efforts during the Meuse-Argonne Offensive of 1918. American soldiers from the 77th Division had pushed too far into the Argonne Forest and became trapped behind German lines. Over 500 men were cut off from reinforcement and supplies. In addition to being fired on by the Germans, they began to receive friendly fire from allied troops who did not know their location. Surrounded by Germans, many of the soldiers were killed and wounded.

Unable to communicate directly, Major Charles Whittlesey and his men began to dispatch carrier pigeons in a desperate attempt to get help. It was their only hope. The pigeon carrying the first message was shot down. A second pigeon was shot down as well. Pigeon after pigeon fell from the sky.

Major Whittlesey ordered the last pigeon to be dispatched. Cher Ami was dispatched with a note in a canister attached to her leg. The note read, "We are along the road parallel to 270.4. Our own military is dropping a barrage directly on us. For heaven's sake stop it." Cher Ami was the last chance the men had to survive.

Cher Ami flew directly into enemy fire, dodging bullets as she went. But shortly after takeoff, she was hit in the chest and fell to the ground. The soldiers were horrified as they saw their last hope disappear.

Although she was severely wounded, Cher Ami somehow got back up. Demonstrating pure will power, she took flight again. Facing wave after wave of gunfire, she flew the 25 miles in approximately 30 minutes. Cher Ami got the message through and helped save the lives of the 194 survivors. She had been shot through the breast, blinded in one eye, and had a leg hanging only by a tendon.

Army medics worked to save Cher Ami's life. They saved her leg by carving a small wooden one for her and attaching it. When she recovered, she was put on a boat for the United States. It's reported that General John J. Pershing personally saw her off and said, "There isn't any way the United States can do too much for this bird."

Cher Ami was awarded France's Croix de Guerre Medal for her gallant service. She died from the wounds she received in battle and was later inducted into the Racing Pigeon Hall of Fame. In addition, she received a gold medal from the Organized Bodies of American Racing Pigeon Fanciers for her heroic effort.

Cher Ami's body was preserved and put on display at the Smithsonian Museum of American History in Washington, D.C. It's difficult to know how many families owe their existence to her courage and sacrifice. Her bravery will never be forgotten.

When I read the article I was impressed with what Cher Ami had done. Her bravery and skill saved 194 men. That's amazing. And then it hit me. I couldn't help but wonder if pigeons might be related to mourning doves. So I did a little research and learned that pigeons and mourning doves do indeed both come from the same bird family called Columbidae. That was a shocking bit of information to me.

At first I didn't know how to handle this information. It forced me to view mourning doves in a different light — a more positive one. I have to admit that it softened my view of mourning doves. Not much, but a little bit. After all, if members of their family could save hundreds of lives, the mourning doves at my feeder couldn't be all bad. I reluctantly decided to lay off my battle with them and let them eat at the feeder.

I guess it just goes to show that things are not always what they seem. I saw the mourning doves as a menace. The military saw them as an important means of communication. I saw them as rather worthless creatures. The military saw them as valuable. I saw them as greedy. The military saw them as sacrificial and brave.

I have to admit, it was difficult for me to change my opinion of mourning doves. After all, change isn't easy. And I still have my moments. When I see those huge overstuffed bodies sitting in my bird feeder devouring my seeds I want to arise from my chair and chase them away. I still struggle when I see them but I grit my teeth and let them eat.

In trying to learn more about doves I came across this quote: "Oh that I had wings like a dove! For then I would fly away and be at rest." (Psalm 55:6) The part I like best about that quote is where it says, "....fly away."

But as I said earlier, things are not always what they seem. It's a good lesson to learn. Don't be so quick to judge. Take the time to know individuals (and birds). Everyone's different. Everyone has value. Accept them for who they are. It may not be easy but it's possible to change.

Thanks to Cher Ami I now have a different view of mourning doves. I guess I'll be buying extra bird seed.

REFLECTION

1. Everything on earth has a purpose. There's a reason that everything exists.
2. Accept people as they are. Don't try to change them to fit what you want them to be. The more you are able to do this, the more peace you will have.
3. *Oh, that I had the wings of a dove! I would fly away and be at rest.* — Psalm 55:6

THE LITTLE GIRL NO ONE WANTED

If there's a song in your heart, sing it.

I don't recall who told me the story about the little girl no one wanted. I just know that it touched me when I heard it and I tucked it away in a corner of my heart for safe keeping. It's one of those stories I like to pull out once in a while and share.

In one of the border skirmishes that the Russians had with the Ukrainians, little six year-old Anna's parents were killed and she was placed in an orphanage.

Americans often visit the Ukraine to find children to adopt. On this one occasion, a group of American couples were at the orphanage talking to the children, hoping to discover at least one child that would appeal to them, one that they could adopt and love and take home to America.

Anna was never chosen. Perhaps it was partly her unkempt appearance. Perhaps it was partly the smudges on her face and hands from making mud pies like her mother used to make with her. Perhaps it was the fact that she was withdrawn and never talked. She didn't rush to the Americans like the other children did, hoping to be chosen. She simply sat on a little chair in the corner, holding the only possession she had from her home, a small rag doll that was as unkempt as she was.

The American couples strolled through the orphanage, studying each child. The children smiled and tried to look their best, hoping to be chosen. The parents walked past Anna, hardly noticing her. In her withdrawn, silent, unkempt appearance, she did not appeal to them.

However, one woman did notice Anna. The woman was a single parent, having lost her husband and young daughter two years earlier in a tragic accident. As a single parent, she thought she had little chance to adopt a child from the orphanage, but she came with the group anyway, her heart full of hope.

The woman brought a beautiful Raggedy Ann doll she had made for her little girl but didn't have a chance to give it to her. She brought it to give to a child in the orphanage. She chose Anna.

She handed the doll to Anna and said, "I want you to have this. Her name is Rebecca."

The lady smiled and gave Anna a hug. Anna smiled back and said, "Thank you." Her voice was almost inaudible.

Soon all the parents gathered in the main room to talk with the orphanage director. They wanted to ask questions about the children before making a final choice.

In the middle of the discussions, the parents suddenly stopped talking and listened to a sound coming from the other room. It was a beautiful sound they had not heard when strolling through the orphanage.

"Who is doing that beautiful singing?"one of the parents asked.

"Oh, that's Anna," the director said. "She talks very little, but she often sings to her doll."

"What an amazing voice," another parent said.

Still another parent replied, "I can't believe a little girl can sing like that."

The parents moved to the other room and stood near Anna and listened. They looked at each other and marveled at Anna's beautiful singing.

The parents were so impressed with Anna that they all wanted to choose her. They now looked past the unkempt appearance and the smudges and saw a little girl with an amazing talent. They each wanted to take her home and love her and nurture her extraordinary talent.

The director went to Anna and said, "Anna, these parents all want you. But I want you to choose which parents you would like to have as your own."

The parents all stood straight, smiled, and hoped to be chosen. Anna looked through the crowd and focused on the small woman who had given her the doll.

"I want her," Anna said.

What a beautiful story. It affirms something I firmly believe. We each have a song within us. But a better name for it is talent, a special gift that is uniquely ours. Its value can only be known if we share it....if we sing it.

When I was in the eighth grade the Wood County Farm Bureau had an essay contest. The topic was conservation. The winner would receive a trip to the Farm Bureau State Convention in Columbus, Ohio. Any student in grades 8 through 12 could enter.

I don't really know why I entered but I did. I knew the odds were against me since I would be competing against many high school students throughout the county. But I enjoyed writing and decided to give it a try.

Somehow I won. I was, of course, quite surprised. I recall that many people said to me, "I didn't know you could write like that." Actually, I didn't either. I just knew I liked it. You might say I discovered that I had a song inside me and decided to "sing it."

To be honest, the best part of the whole night was the delicious chocolate dessert that I had for dinner. I had never had it before. One of the gentlemen at the table was on a diet so he gave me his dessert. I was in heaven. Two desserts. That really made my heart sing.

REFLECTION

1. A song is good therapy. There's one for every feeling, every mood, every situation.
2. Within you is a favorite song. Sing it and be filled with nostalgia, comfort and joy.
3. *Sing and make music in your heart.* — Ephesians 5:18

WHAT MAKES A PERSON LIKABLE?

People like genuine people.

There's a song we used to sing growing up that went like this:
"Nobody likes me. Everybody hates me. I think I'll go eat worms. Big fat juicy ones. Wee little slimy ones. See how they wiggle and squirm. Bite their heads off. Suck their juice out. Throw their skins away. No one knows how I can live on worms three times a day."

I think everyone has moments when they get down on themselves and feel like nobody likes them. But they want to be liked. They may not know what to do to be likable but they wish to be. Of course, wishing doesn't make it happen. It takes a lot of self-awareness.

Studies have shown there are certain qualities that make a person likable. They're practical qualities anyone can achieve. Here's a summary of some of them.

- They make you feel good when you are with them.
- They're friendly.
- They greet you with a smile.
- When you talk with them they give you their undivided attention. They make you feel like they want to hear what you have to say.
- They genuinely care about you.
- They're encouraging and give compliments.
- They're willing to give feedback when asked but are not judgmental and do not criticize.

- They're open minded. They allow others to have their own opinions.
- They're warm, kind and considerate.
- They apologize when they are wrong or make mistakes.
- They practice forgiveness.
- They're optimistic and upbeat,
- They're reliable.
- They're fun to be around.

Think of a person that you find likable. How many of these qualities does the person have?

I know I can personally do better at some of these qualities. But I don't want to do it just to be liked. I want to do it because it will make me a better person. That's the bottom line.

REFLECTION

1. Rather than focusing on being likable, focus on being yourself.
2. Like me or leave me, I like the wonderful, unique work of art that I am.
3. *I know the plans I have for you, plans to prosper you and not to harm you, plans to give you hope and a future.* — Jeremiah 29:11

THINGS TO DO AND NOT DO
WHEN SOMEONE IS HURTING

Remember, when someone's hurting, it's about them, not you.

When you're hurting, it's healing to know that others are hurting for you and with you. It's comforting when someone says, "I understand," and they take the time to be there for you in a supportive way. They might run an errand for you or drop off a meal or do something else that they know will be of help to you. They don't have to ask; they simply go ahead and do it.

On the other hand, when someone is hurting, it's not so helpful to say, "Let me know if there's anything I can do for you." Even if you mean well, it comes across as rather hollow, especially when there's always something you can do. It doesn't matter how big or small, just go ahead and do it. It will help the healing. If nothing else, send a note of encouragement, or spend time with the person. Take them out to lunch, maybe bake or buy them some cookies. Give them a gift card to a restaurant that you know they like. Be creative. Think of things that would be uniquely meaningful to that person.

Perhaps the most healing thing you can do is just be present with them. If you can't be there physically, make a phone call. Be present not just during a crisis, but in the long term as well. Sometimes when people have suffered a painful crisis, they need you most in the weeks and months after it takes place. Stay connected. It will mean the world to them, and it will bless you as well.

REFLECTION

1. When someone is hurting, a simple hug is often more important than words. It's the little things, like a hug, that will long occupy a major part of their heart.
2. When people are hurting, what they often need the most is for someone to simply be present with them. Support them by spending time with them. Just be there.
3. *When you go through deep waters, I will be with you.* —Isaiah 43:2

PARABLE OF THE EMPEROR'S SEEDS

If you want to be trusted, be honest.

I love parables. I appreciate how a simple story can illustrate a powerful moral or spiritual lesson. It's amazing how a brief tale, sometimes just a paragraph or two, can illustrate a profound universal truth.

One of my favorite parables is about an emperor in the Far East who was growing old and weak. He decided to call all the children in the kingdom together and choose one of them as his successor.

He got them together and said, "I'm going to give each of you a seed and a pot to put it in. Plant the seed and come back in six months with what you have grown. I will choose the child with the best plant to be my successor.

A small girl named Lia went home and planted her seed. She watered it faithfully but nothing happened. Weeks went by and still nothing happened. She heard the other children talking about how beautiful their plants were and she felt sad. She felt like she had failed.

A year went by and the emperor called for the children to bring their plants in for him to judge. Lia cried because she had nothing to present. Her mother told her she had done what was requested and should return her pot to the emperor.

Lia set her pot on the floor amidst all the beautiful plants brought by the other children. The other children laughed at her empty pot.

The emperor examined all the plants. Lia explained to him that she did what was requested but nothing grew. She apologized for being a failure.

After all the plants were examined, the emperor said, "Behold, your new emperor. Her name is Lia." The crowd was stunned. After all, Lia couldn't grow a seed, how could she be emperor.

Then the emperor said, "I gave each of you a seed, but the seeds were dead. I had them boiled so they wouldn't grow. All of you except Lia placed a plant in the pot hoping to deceive me. Lia is the only honest one. Therefore, Lia is the new emperor."

This is such a powerful lesson. I'm guessing everyone has had moments when they struggled with dishonesty.

I taught high school English when I first graduated from college. I was surprised at the number of students who attempted to cheat on an exam. They were good kids from good families. They each had their own reason for cheating. I spent time privately with each one I caught cheating and tried to draw good out of their dishonest actions. I wanted to make it a learning situation. Some explained that they felt pressure to get a good grade. Others shared that they simply hadn't studied and cheating was an easy way out. All of them expressed regret and were relieved that I was not going to involve their parents. Spending time talking with them about the importance of integrity seemed to help as the cheating subsided significantly.

One group act of deception was rather humorous. One day I entered the classroom and sat on the chair at my desk. I felt pain. I realized immediately that I had sat on a sharp thumb tack. I stood and looked at the students. I could tell they were all part of "the plot." I asked if anyone would like to be honest and admit placing the tack on the chair. No one said a word. I asked if anyone knew who did it. Still silence.

I said, "Fine. We'll all sit in silence until someone admits to placing the tack on the chair. We will sit in silence for as many days as it takes." There was laughter. They thought it was funny. But their laughter turned to concern when I said, "And at the end of each class period whereby no one admits to placing the tack on the chair, I will give everyone an F." Immediately the heads all turned and looked at one young man who happened to be one of my brightest and most respected students. He raised his hand and admitted to doing it.

I had a long talk with the whole class. I told them that placing the tack on the chair was a prank. But the whole class denying that they knew who did it was deception. We had a good discussion and I think everyone learned a lot about deception and its consequences. What they didn't know was I probably would never have given everyone an F. I would not have felt comfortable doing it.

I also learned from the situation. I learned that as a teacher your best lessons don't always come from your lesson plan. It helps to be flexible.

REFLECTION

1. A person who has integrity will win the respect of others.
2. Always be clear about your standards. Be honest with people about who you are, what you want, what you stand for, and how you expect to be treated.
3. *For we are taking pains to do what is right, not only in the eyes of the Lord, but also in the eyes of men.* —2 Corinthians 8:21

DISCOVER THE SWEETNESS OF LIFE

Take the time to taste life's nectar.

I wake up early, sometimes as early as 4:00 a.m. I enjoy getting up, getting my cup of coffee, and going outside to the back patio or my meditation garden to watch dawn arrive.

One morning, as dawn kissed the morning dew, I noticed a flash of rainbow lightning with iridescent wings darting and diving from flower to flower. What a treat to start my day, observing a dancing, dazzling hummingbird that had come my way.

As I watched this wonder of nature, dozens of words dashed through my mind that seemed to capture what I saw the dancing hummingbird so adeptly doing — darting, dashing, discovering, and finally drinking the sweet nectar of flowers.

Oh, that my day should go as well, I thought. Oh, that I might also search for, discover, and appreciate all that flowers around me and taste life's sweet nectar. Oh that I might taste and savor the sweetness that life offers.

I guess it's the educator in me, but I love to draw lessons out of what I encounter in life. I'm always asking myself questions like, "What does this mean to me?" "What lesson can I draw out of this?" I rarely just see an object. I have to draw meaning out of what I see.

As I watched the hummingbird that morning, thoughts about life buzzed through my mind, all positive. I think what I learned the most from watching the hummingbird was this: Each day focus on sipping life's sweet nectar. Look for the sweet moments in life and taste them.

Nature has a way, like nothing else, to make us feel good. It's like medicine to the soul and peace to the mind. It invites us to enjoy the beauty that thousands of years have created for us. It invites us to examine its mysterious ways, listen to its sounds, and touch its textures. Nature gives us so much, teaches us so many things. It truly is the world's greatest classroom.

REFLECTION

1. All of nature grows in silence. The universe moves in silence. Perhaps silence is something we should value more in our own lives.
2. Don't be afraid of change. Nature teaches us that it's normal, natural, and necessary.
3. *But ask the beasts, and they will teach you; the birds of the heavens, and they will tell you; or the bushes of the earth, and they will teach you; and the fish of the sea will declare to you. Who among all of these does not know that the Lord has done this?* (Job 12:7-10)

GET A BUCKET AND MAKE A LIST

Always maintain a pocket full of dreams.

Everyone needs a bucket list. It's simply a list of things you would like to experience in life before you die. Most people think about things they would like to do, but they don't write them down.

Why make a bucket list? It's simply to remind yourself of things, big and small, that are important enough to you to want to experience. It's not a "to do" list. There is no pressure to get it done. Its value is that it helps give you a sense of purpose. It gives your life direction, without demands or agenda. It sets forth your hopes and dreams. It's not set in stone. You can make changes and adjust it as you go. There's no failure associated with the list. It doesn't matter if you achieve one item on the list or all of them. It's simply to give your life focus. Every item you cross off your list makes your life more satisfying.

A study by Dr. V. J. Periyakoil, an associate professor at Stanford's medical school, surveyed over 3,000 patients to find out what was on their bucket list as a way to get to know them better. She discovered the information helped her come up with treatment plans that better addressed what her patients wanted out of their lives. The results showed that people's items on their bucket list tended to fall into one of several broad categories:

- Travel
- Accomplish a person goal
- Achieve a milestone like get married or see a grandchild's birth
- Spend quality time with friends and family

- Achieve financial stability
- Do a daring activity

A separate study also listed:

- Hobbies
- Spiritual growth
- Volunteering

I was surprised at what the research showed. For example, people who have a bucket list, a defined purpose in life, tend to live longer than those who do not. According to a study done by Dr. Stephanie Hooker and published in the *Review of General Psychology,* people with a sense of purpose tend to have a healthier, happier, more meaningful life. If it means living longer, that's one very good reason to have a bucket list.

The live stage production of *The Lion King* had been on my bucket list for a long time. I love the movie as well as the music. But over the years no traveling Broadway production of the show came to Tallahassee, where I live, or to any city nearby. I kept it on my list because it was something I really wanted to experience.

A few months ago, my sister-in-law from Bradenton, Florida, called and said *The Lion King* stage production was coming to Sarasota, Florida. Did we want tickets? We of course said, "Yes!" I could hardly wait for the event to take place. When the date arrived, we traveled to Sarasota to view the show with her. I wasn't disappointed. It was everything I had heard it would be and more.

I have to say, *The Lion King,* in my mind, is one of the most creative stage productions ever produced. From the first scene to the last, it's simply a stunning, mind-boggling array of creativity. It made everything seem fresh and new and unique. It made everything interesting and fascinating. Wow.

That's how I think our lives should be lived, no matter what our age is. Our lives should be a stunning, mind-boggling array of creativity. We should live in such a way that everything is fresh and new and unique. We should do everything we can to make life interesting and fascinating.

REFLECTION

1. One of the most important things you can do is cross off completed items from your bucket list.
2. Too many people leave this life with their music still in them and their dreams unfulfilled. Be the exception.
3. *May he give you the desire of your heart and make all your plans succeed.* — Psalm 20:4

THE SIX MINUTE WALK TEST

Failure doesn't mean you quit.
It means you get to try again.

I was surprised when the cardiologist said, "I'm going to send you to have a Six Minute Walk Test. It's a test that will give us a good assessment of how your lungs are functioning."

"I've never been a good test taker," I said. "And if it has anything to do with aerobics, I'll fail for sure. I once failed junior high gym and all we did was stand around and do nothing."

"It has nothing to do with aerobics," he said. "And it's not something you pass or fail. All you do is get on a treadmill and take a leisurely six minute walk. That's all there is to it. It's a piece of cake."

"You make it sound easy," I said. "But I want you to know that just last spring I was talked into going on a Heart Walk to raise funds for heart research. It was supposed to be just a little walk, maybe five or six minutes. But it was 95 degree weather and no shade and I almost didn't make it. I have to tell you it was like a "death march.""

The doctor reassured me that the six minute walk was easy. He said it was inside in air conditioning and not it sweltering heat. That made me feel better.

A few days later I returned to the clinic for my Six Minute Walk Test. I was greeted with a smile by the attendant and ushered through wide double doors, down a long hallway, and finally was told to sit down in what appeared to be a mini-waiting room. A matronly lady, about sixty-five years old, was sitting there reading a magazine. I never read magazines in waiting rooms because I once read that there are more germs on every single page of a magazine that's been there more than a month than there is on the average kitchen dish cloth.

Why anyone would research something like that I'll never know, but it made me leery of touching the waiting room magazines. And it also makes me wonder about germs on kitchen dish cloths.

When I sat down, the lady reading the magazine said, "Getting old isn't for sissies."

Right or wrong, I had not yet reached that stage in my life where I considered myself to be "old," so I wondered why she assumed I was in that category. I realized I was getting "older," but I didn't see myself as "old." Not that I see anything wrong with being "old." In fact, I think it can be a wonderful age. I just didn't see myself being there yet.

"All these tests they put you through don't help any either," she said. "Have you had this here walk test before?"

I wasn't sure I wanted to get drawn into a conversation, but I said, "No, this is my first time."

"I was just in that little room an hour ago," she said. "Believe me, it's so small it's claustrophobic. And warm, too. I thought I was going to pass out."

Visions of my "death march" in 95 degree heat went through my head and I said, "Warm? How warm was it?"

"It wasn't just warm, it was hot," she said. "It felt like there was no air conditioning. And there are no windows. It was more like a closet with a treadmill crammed into it. I'm telling you, it was claustrophobic. They told me I could stop at any point if I had to, so I did. After just one minute. I thought I would then get to go home, but they told me to come back here and sit for a while and then I would have to do it again. I'm prone to having panic attacks and I'm sitting here about to have one just thinking about going back in there."

Before I could respond, I heard a man's voice yell, "Stop!" followed by some rumbling, and then the door to the walking closet opened and a chubby man wearing bib overalls came out. His face was red and sweaty. He came directly to the little waiting room huffing and puffing, sat down, reached under his chair, and pulled out a bag that he had apparently left there. He unzipped the bag and pulled out a Hershey's candy bar and, with shaky hands, unwrapped it and took a big bite.

"I've got to have some sugar or I'm gonna pass out," he said.

"Did you make it through this time?" the claustrophobic lady asked.

The man took another big bite of his candy bar and said, "No, just four minutes worth. They told me to come out here and wait. I don't know if I'll have to do it again or not."

The door opened and I heard my name called.

"Please come this way," the young lady said, as she looked me over, which made me feel like she was maybe sizing me up to see if I was going to be a wimp or a track star.

We entered what was definitely a small room, barely big enough for a large treadmill. For some reason it reminded me of the great white shark, "Jaws," quietly waiting to swallow its next victim. I wouldn't say this to the claustrophobic lady out there in the waiting room about to have a panic attack, but that darned treadmill actually looked like something alive and breathing. I shouldn't watch horror movies.

"Please sit here," the young lady said, pointing to the only chair in the room."Have you had this test before?"She looked very young to me, maybe too young to be very experienced, but then I thought how everyone looks young to me these days.

"No, I haven't," I said. But I wanted to tell her I was an experienced zombie who recently walked a death march in 95 degree heat. This would be a piece of cake.

"Well, here's what I'm going to do," she said. "I'm going to put a few patches on your chest to monitor your heart, a blood pressure cuff on your arm to keep an eye on your blood pressure, and attach a pulse oximeter to your finger that will measure your oxygen saturation and pulse. I'm also going to put a shunt in your hand so I can give you nuclear injections while you walk."

"Nuclear injections?" I said. "Isn't that a little dangerous?"

She just smiled and said, "It's very safe."

I was more than a little nervous as she began to prepare me for my encounter with Jaws. "And I'm supposed to be able to walk with all of these attachments on me and with you giving me injections?" I said. "How many people actually survive this simple walk test?"

She smiled again. "Most people do just fine. You just have to have a good mind-set about it."

"I think it takes more than that," I said. "Like powerful athletic legs, which I don't have, and the ability to multi-task, which I've never been good at either."

"You'll do fine," she said. Now, just step up on the treadmill and picture something pleasant and peaceful as you walk. Are you ready?"

All I could picture in my mind were those two people in the waiting room who failed the test. Before I could come up with anything pleasant and peaceful to envision, I heard the door behind me open and shut.

"The cardiologist is here, so we're ready to go," the technician said, and then turned on the treadmill. There were now three of us in that small room, without windows, and the heat in the room was rising by the minute. The cardiologist was standing somewhere behind me. I was certain that he didn't want to be seen laughing at this scene. My legs were now moving whether I wanted them to or not.

"I'm now going to inject the adenosine," the tech said. "You might feel some slight nausea, shortness of breath, facial flushing, or dizziness, but it won't last long."

She made the injection and then said, "How are you doing?"

"I think I feel some nausea, shortness of breath, facial flushing, and a slight dizziness," I said. "I'm one of those people who reads all the side-effects of prescription medications and immediately experiences the symptoms."

She laughed and I also heard the cardiologist laugh. So I laughed also. We all had a good laugh.....on me. It was funny until I felt my-out-of-shape legs start to weaken.

"How many more minutes?" I asked.

"We're not even half-way there," she said. "I still have another injection to give you."

"My legs are turning to rubber," I said. "Are you increasing the tempo?"

"No, not at all," she said. "It's going at a nice easy pace."

I was certain that she had increased the speed because Jaws and I were now flying through the wide blue sea.

She gave me the last injection and asked, "How do you feel?"

"Well, I can't feel my legs," I said. "Are they still there?"

Perhaps it was the power of suggestion, but the symptoms she described earlier hit me all at once for real: shortness of breath, dizziness, nausea, sweating. You name it, I was experiencing it. I now realized why the man in the bib overalls came out of the room sweating with a red face, and why the lady felt claustrophobic. The room was closing in on me. I was going to fail this simple piece-of-cake test. I just knew I would have to do a repeat.

"I don't think I can make it," I said, between gasps for air.

"You can do it," the tech said. "You're almost there."

My mind flashed back to my death march for the Heart Walk and how I somehow made it to the finish line. I told myself if I could do that I could do this. Then I heard a beautiful sound: a little bell rang and the treadmill stopped.

"You made it," the tech said. "Congratulations."

"Good job," the cardiologist said and left the room.

The tech helped me and my rubber legs off the treadmill and said, "Go sit in the waiting room and I'll be with you in a minute. Do you need help getting there?"

"No, I think I can make it," I said, as I tried to get both legs moving in the same direction.

I wobbled to the waiting room and slumped in a chair. I looked at the red-faced man who was now eating a Snickers candy bar. "Do you happen to have another one of those Snickers?" I asked. "I think I need some sugar."

"Sure do," he said. "Got a bunch of them in my bag."

He reached in, got one, and handed it to me. I looked at the claustrophobic lady who was also now eating a candy bar. I held up my candy bar and said, "Here's to you both. If I did the six-minute walk, you can too. You're going to make it."

Before I left the clinic that day I learned that they both had completed the six-minute walk. I was reminded of that old saying, "Failure doesn't mean you quit. It means you get to try again."

REFLECTION

1. It's not having a strong desire to win that makes you a winner, it's refusing to give up when you fail that causes you to succeed.

2. Success in life comes when you refuse to give up. When your determination to reach your goals is so strong that obstacles, failure and loss only act as motivation.

3. *He gives strength to the weary and increases the power of the weak. Even youths grow tired and weary, and the young stumble and fall; but those who hope in the Lord will renew their strength. They will soar on wings like eagles; they will run and not grow weary, they will walk and not be faint.* — Isaiah 40:29-31

IT'S NEVER TOO LATE TO DREAM

When you put your dreams in writing, they became goals.

It's never too late to dream. If your heart is still beating, there's still time for dreams. There's still time to follow your heart and walk down a new path. There's still time to do what you've always wanted to do.

This might surprise you but there's still time to have a happy childhood. The child in you is still alive. Do things the child in you always wanted to do. It doesn't matter how silly or foolish the things might seem. You might have to modify it somewhat, but do it to whatever degree you can.

Be creative. If you always wanted to enter a spelling bee, get a few friends together and have a spelling bee. If you always wanted to ride the world's tallest roller coaster, do some research where one is located and go do it. Be creative. You can still have a happy childhood.

One of the things I wanted to do as a child was write silly poems about silly classmates. I told myself I would do it someday. When I retired that "someday" came. I told myself I was 75 years old (at the time) and it was time to do it. I wanted to let that child in me finally express himself and fulfill that little dream I had had for so long. That little child in me ended up writing 26 silly poems, one for each letter of the alphabet. Here is one of them to give you an idea of how I did something the little child in me always wanted to do. It's one I wrote for the alphabet letter <u>M</u>.

Everyone knows that **M**yron **M**ears
Never washes behind his ears,

and little creatures gather there.
They even crawl into his hair.
The other children often stare;
but Myron says he doesn't care.
He likes his dirty ears and hair,
and the little bugs that gather there.

There's also still time to have a joyful, adventurous adulthood and do the things you always wanted to do. If you always wanted to have a small business, you can still do it. If you always wanted to learn to dance, you can still do it. If you always wanted to take a cruise, do it. If you always wanted to ride a horse down a lonesome trail, rent a horse and do it. If you always wanted to travel to Europe, you can still do it. If there's a desire, there's a way to make dreams happen.

Almost everyone knows the story of Ray Kroc. Born of Czech immigrant parents, Kroc started as a milkshake mixer salesman. He was impressed by the McDonald brothers' six hamburger restaurants. He had sold several milkshake mixers to them. He dreamed about being a part of the business someday and he envisioned how the business might go nation-wide. In 1955, when he was 53, he purchased a franchise from the brothers. He then bought out the brothers in 1961. He never gave up on his dream to go nationwide and continued to open more and more restaurants. At the time of his death, he had 7,500 outlets in 31 countries with a net worth of $600 million.

It's not too late to make your dream happen. Colonel Sanders was 62 when he started Kentucky Fried Chicken. Henry Bernstein wrote his first book at 93. Gladys Burrill ran her first marathon race at the age of 92. Roget published his first *"Roget's Thesaurus of English Words and Phrases,"* at age 73. Chaleo Yoovidhya was 61 when he started Red Bull. Charles Ranlett Flint launched IBM at age 61. Jim Butenschoen was 65 when he founded Career Academy of Hair Design, and Radha Daga was 73 when she started Triguni Foods. This is just a sampling of individuals who had a dream and refused to let age be a limiting factor.

Anybody can get on this list. It doesn't have to be big dreams. It's simply choosing to do something you really would like to do. Someone once said, "It's not the age, it's the vision. It's all about having the dream."

One of my dreams for a long time was to be able to do oil painting and perhaps someday have an art show. Once I finally retired (for the fourth time), at the age of 79, I bought some oil paints, brushes, and canvases, set up an art studio in my home office, and started painting. I loved it. I painted almost daily for over a year. I started posting my paintings on Facebook to share them with my relatives and friends. One day my niece from Ohio, who had seen the paintings online, called and asked if I would like to bring my paintings to Ohio and do an art show. I was so surprised, yet I was thrilled with the opportunity.

I was also hesitant because I wasn't sure my paintings were art show quality. But my niece talked me into it. My wife, Muriel, prepared the paintings, all 120 pieces, with frames and backings. In June, 2018, we drove to Ohio and held the art show in one of my other niece's gift shop, *Calico, Sage and Thyme*, in Bowling Green, Ohio. It was such a joy to experience the art show, and at 80 years of age, my dream was realized. It can happen. It's never too late to make dreams happen.

Some people say it helps to write your dream down on one or more cards and place them where you will see them every day, such as in a book you're reading, taped on the bathroom mirror, or some other conspicuous place. The idea is to do what you have to do to keep your dream alive so you can think about ways to make it happen.

It takes creative thinking to form your dreams and be able to get a clear vision of what you really want to do. Perhaps the most important thing to do is get a clear vision of what your dream is and decide you really want to pursue it. Having the vision and having the desire are half the battle.

REFLECTION

1. Dream big. If you believe it's possible, it can happen.
2. You become what you believe. You pursue what you dream.
3. *Your young men shall see visions, your old men shall dream dreams.* — Acts 2:17

QUALITIES OF INDIVIDUALS WHO ACHIEVE THEIR GOALS

The happiest people are those who pursue happiness.

I'm a dreamer. I like to set goals and go after them. It gives my life purpose to be working toward something I want to achieve. I enjoy small goals, such as wanting to construct a flower bed, as much as I enjoy large goals, such as pursuing an advanced degree in college.

When Muriel and I sat down to decide whether or not I should pursue a doctoral degree in counseling, we knew it would take a lot of sacrifice and effort to attempt such a major goal. We had three small children at the time and that weighed in on the discussion. We didn't treat the subject lightly. We were determined that if we did it we would be fully committed to achieving our goal. We wouldn't quit in the middle of the program.

Once I was accepted into the doctoral program, we agreed there would be no dropping out. However, that wasn't true with many of the students in the doctoral program with me. I was stunned to see so many of them quit the program. I was surprised to learn that, statistically, only 25% of the doctoral students finish the program. To say it another way, 75% of the doctoral students do not reach their goal.

Various studies indicate there are certain qualities people seem to have who set goals and accomplish them. It's interesting information. I had never thought much about what it takes to reach a goal. I just did it. But what I learned seems to make sense. Here are three key qualities of people who reach their goals.

1. They have an "I can do it" winning attitude.

They are determined to give their best at what they do. Their outlook is optimistic. They feel positive and confident about what they can accomplish. While working as an engineer for the Edison Illuminating Company in Detroit, Henry Ford built his first gasoline-powered horseless carriage in the shed behind his home. He was determined to build an automobile. He told himself he could do it. In 1903 he established the Ford Motor Company and five years later the company rolled out the first Model T automobile. He did it!

2. They keep learning and growing.
    They're not content to settle for where they are in life or what they've learned. They have a hunger to keep learning, to find ways to improve what they're doing and who they are. They're passionate about doing better. They're examples of the wise saying: *"Growth is the difference between those who succeed and those who do not."* Benjamin Franklin was an American scientist, inventor, politician, philanthropist and business man. He helped draft the Declaration of Independence and the U.S. Constitution. He was constantly investigating and learning. He was fascinated about electricity. He learned everything he could about the topic. He is given credit for discovering the basics of electricity. He never stopped learning.

3. They persevere.
    They have a focus and they don't waiver from it. They're resilient, unwilling to give up. Their willpower is strong. When they get knocked down, they don't stay down. They get back up and keep going. At the age of 13 and a rising surf star, Bethany Hamilton lost her left arm to a 14-foot tiger shark. People thought it would end her career. But within two years she returned to surfing and won her first national surfing title. She refused to give up.

What's interesting about these qualities is they're actually goals. Each one is something to strive for, something to attain. I looked at these qualities and decided that I needed to continue to grow in each one of them, some more than others. I chose the one I needed to work on the most and am working on it. I'm determined to improve.

What's also interesting is that all of these qualities are reasonable for anyone to incorporate into their lives. They're qualities anyone can achieve, young or older.

REFLECTION

1. Perhaps more important than the achievement of your goal is how it makes you feel as a person.
2. All successful people have a goal. No one can get anywhere unless he knows where he wants to go and what he wants to be or do. — Norman Vincent Peals
3. *Let us not be weary in doing good for we will reap in due season, if we don't give up.* (Gal. 6:9)

MAKE SOMETHING GOOD HAPPEN BETWEEN "HELLO" AND "GOODBYE"

Never miss the opportunity to share special time with those you love.

The older I get the faster time seems to go. I once heard someone say, "Time may last forever, but life does not." How true that statement is. So often it seems like I have just said "*hello*" to someone and it's time to say "*goodbye*." It makes me realize how important it is to take advantage of the time between "hello" and "goodbye" and use it well. It prompts me to make a greater effort to keep in touch with family and friends.

Actually, there's no excuse to not be in touch with people in today's world. Technology provides us with a wide variety of communication tools. Skype is just one example. I sometimes wonder how I ever got along without it. In my humble opinion, Skype is one of the greatest inventions of all time. It's like a modern day communication miracle. And the amazing thing is it doesn't cost a cent to use. It simply doesn't come any better than that.

The ingenious, creative individuals who created Skype have made it possible for the whole world to connect with each other like never before. In my humble opinion, what they did ranks up there with Henry Ford, the Wright brothers, Alexander Graham Bell, and Thomas Edison.

I did a little research and learned that Skype was created in 2003 by Swede Niklas Zennstrom and Dane Janus Friis in cooperation with Estonians Ahti

Heinla, Priit Kasesalu and Jaan Tallinn. This amazing invention allows users to communicate over the internet by voice using a microphone, by video using a webcam, and by instant messaging. It was purchased just two years later by eBay in 2005 for $2.6 billion. Wow. Not a bad profit. Microsoft bought it in 2011 for $8.5 billion. Another wow! Skype claims over 700 million worldwide users. It's mind- boggling.

I am not a "techie." Never ask me to fix your computer. All I know is that Skype makes it possible for Muriel and me to see and talk to our daughter and son-in-law in Cincinnati, our daughter and son-in-law in New Zealand, and our son and daughter-in-law in Chicago. We feel fortunate to have one son who lives here in Tallahassee. We can communicate with him the old fashioned way — in person.

Skype also allows us to keep in touch with our grandchildren and great grandchildren and see the expressions on their faces as we chat. It's like sitting in the living room and having an up-close conversation with them. What a wonderful contribution to the world these individuals made.

When I was in the eighth grade, there was a large clock on the wall in the room where I had English class. Of course, as students will do, we glanced at the clock often, hoping the class period would go fast and soon be over. I think our teacher got tired of us glancing at the clock. One day when we entered the classroom, we saw that the teacher had put a large sign on the wall beside the clock. It stated, "Time will pass, will you?"

I got the point. It was cleverly presented by our teacher and I have always remembered it. Time will pass....and pass quickly. Will I use the "*in between*" time wisely and make good things happen?

It's definitely a challenge to look at each of the key people in one's life and think about what you can do in each relationship to make good things happen between the "*hellos*" and the "*goodbyes*." It takes time and effort to determine what unique things you can do to keep each relationship alive. Of course, all relationships are different and what works for one may not work for another. You have to be creative in your thinking. But here's the thing, even the smallest effort can make a difference. You don't always have to do a major overhaul.

I guess the bottom line is this: don't delay in doing what you need to do to make your relationships better. Remember, life passes in the blink of an eye. The opportunity you have today to improve a relationship may not be available tomorrow.

As for the journey we have taken through this book, I hope it has lifted your spirits as it has mine. As we said at the beginning, "these are the times that try men's souls." Life in today's world is full of challenges. "For such a time as this" encouragement is needed to get through the tough times.

Someone once told me that one of the greatest gifts we can give another person is a word of encouragement. I believe that's true. We must never underestimate the power of encouragement and what it can do for someone.

I hope you will take the time to reflect on the 9 themes that were presented in this book and apply the ones that will help you grow as a person. Listed below is a summary of the themes and some practical suggestions for you to consider — just a few thoughts to get you started:

1. Laugh often — laughter is good medicine that makes you feel better.
   - First thing each morning, look in the mirror and smile. No matter how groggy or sleepy you are or how resistant you are to smiling, do your best to make it happen. Just as you sometimes have to jump start the battery in your car to get it running, the same is true for your face. You might have to jump start it with a hot cup of coffee or tea. However you do it, smile. It will have a positive effect on your whole day. I promise.
   - No matter what you experienced yesterday or what you face today, be determined to smile. Tell yourself you are in charge and you are not going to allow any person or anything prevent you from having an uplifting day.
   - Studies show that each time you smile you throw "a little feel good party in your brain." It's true. Smiling activates neural messaging that benefits your health and happiness. So when you smile, the guys in your brain get to have a party. Don't let them down.
   - Studies also show that your smile encourages others. If you smile at someone, it's likely they can't help but smile back. I've tried this and it works. In the grocery store I like to catch the eye of fellow shoppers and smile. And guess what? Most of them smile back. My smile helps to jump start their day.
   - Different from the smile is the laugh. And it's just as important. It involves a giggle or a chuckle. If nothing during the day makes

you laugh, get online and Google "joke of the day." Keep reading until you find one that makes you laugh. Trust me, this works.

- Here's the good news: according to research, laughter can improve memory, improve immunity, help regulate blood sugar levels, and improve sleep. All good reasons to laugh.
- In the best of times and the worst of times, it helps to laugh because it lifts your spirits.

2. Learn from nature, the world's greatest classroom — it teaches all you need to know about how to live life, maintain balance, and survive.
   - Take the time to enjoy nature. Soak in all the benefits it offers you.
   - There are so many aspects to nature, so much to choose from and enjoy. You can easily find something about nature that fits your interests. You get to choose what appeals to you.
   - For example, if you like hiking, do it. If you enjoy watching nature shows on television, watch and learn. If you like fishing, "go fish." If gardening is your thing, plant and cultivate vegetables and flowers and watch them grow. If you enjoy sitting by a peaceful body of water and reflecting, by all means do it. If you want to find a getaway spot where you can look and listen to the unique sights and sounds of nature, do it.
   - The point is, it's encouraging to spend time in nature because it's not only fascinating, it offers a change of pace from the hustle-bustle of life. It has a way of soothing the soul and putting your mind at ease.
   - Studies show that being in nature, or even viewing scenes of nature (like a calendar), reduces anger, fear, and stress, increases pleasant feelings, and improves mood.
   - There's something very encouraging about nature because in its own mysterious way it makes you feel better.

3. Do the things that make you feel young at heart — have fun, imagine, explore, play, sing, dance, jump rope, go to the circus, eat cotton candy.
   - Feel free to act a little squirrely at times. You'll be surprised at how much you enjoy it. Give the child within you permission to let loose and have fun.

- You'll find that it's quite healing to let loose and do something silly.
- It's even better to do something silly with a family member or friend. It could be as silly as eating cake with your fingers. Maybe you and a friend could wear your tee-shirt inside out. Ever get with several others and try to lick your nose with your tongue? It's a barrel of fun. Send someone a text and say something silly and innocuous, like, "The butterflies have arrived. Where do you want them?"
- Allow yourself to have fun. But remember, never do anything at someone else's expense.
- Here's something you might want to know. Studies show that people who are playful appear to be better at coping with stress, lead more active lifestyles, are more attractive to others and are more likely to succeed academically.
- Feeling the freedom to do something silly and allowing yourself to have fun will lift your spirits because freedom is encouraging.

4. Share your love and treat others the way you want to be treated.
    - Choose to reach out and love those who need and want your love. They will appreciate it.
    - Find meaningful ways to show people in your life that you love them. Doing little things that are unique and personal works best, especially when they're done as a surprise.
    - Do random acts of kindness anonymously. When I was young I use to get my dad's "dress shoes" out of his closet and shine them, especially when I knew he was going to be wearing them the next day. He never said anything, but I loved the look on his face when he saw them.
    - Try writing down a favorite memory you've had with someone and leave it where they can find it.
    - Put in writing the good qualities you see in a person and mail it to them. It will make them feel so special.
    - Studies show that communicating affection has such health benefits as lower stress hormones, lower cholesterol, lower blood

pressure, and a stronger immune system. Sharing your love makes a difference.

- There's nothing more encouraging than giving love and receiving it.

5. Focus on things that really matter in life — let go of the rest.
   - Make a list. I know it's not everyone's favorite thing to do. But lists do make a difference. Studies have shown that people perform better when they write down what they plan to do.
   - So get your pencil out and make a list of what really matters to you. Be serious about it. Give a lot of thought to it. Put the list on your refrigerator or wherever you can see it daily. It helps to see it.
   - Research indicates that when you focus on what really matters you will get more accomplished, your work will have higher quality, and you will feel less stress.
   - If you like, here's an extra thing you can do that's fun. At the end of each week, put on the bottom of the sheet the number (on a scale of 1 to 10) that best indicates how you did staying focused on the things that really matter to you. It helps you keep focused.
   - It's encouraging to know that your life has meaning and you are making an effort to focus on the things that are important to you.

6. Strengthen the bridges in your relationships — build new ones if necessary.
   - Do the things you know will strengthen the important relationships in your life.
   - Choose the relationship in your life that you want to work on the most and focus your energy on it. It's best to work on one at a time.
   - Be realistic and honest about the relationship. Identify the specific things that need to be improved and then work on them one at a time.
   - Don't try to change the other person by saying things like, "You need to do this or you need to do that." Keep your focus on what *you* personally can do to improve the relationship. And remember, you improve relationships by being an encourager, not a critic. As you work on the relationship, be patient. Be kind. Do all things in love. Remember, you're building bridges, not tearing them down.

- You will be surprised at how encouraged you will feel when the relationship you are working on begins to improve.
- The benefits of a strong relationship are amazing. Studies show that those who are in a strong relationship are happier, tend to live longer, heal quicker, have lower blood pressure, have a stronger immune system, and better heart health. These are good reasons to build strong relationships.

7. Believe in the creative spirit that's within you and give yourself permission to express it.
   - Start by accepting the fact that you do, indeed, have a creative spirit within you. It's God-given. You've always had it. Think about all the ways you expressed it as a child.
   - Just as you did as a child, explore your creative spirit as an adult and find ways to express it in a personally meaningful way and unique to you.
   - Take the time to determine what you would enjoy doing that would be some form of creative expression
   - Remember, the sky's the limit. For example, you could construct a wood project, You might choose to spend time gardening. Perhaps you enjoy music and could sing in a choir. You might want to try sewing, crocheting, or knitting, Writing daily in a journal can be very creative, Maybe you always wanted to sketch or paint, People don't realize that playing games or doing puzzles is very creative. You might want to try your hand at writing poetry. An easy creative thing to do is to take classes. It's also easy to travel or volunteer or read a book. The list is endless.
   - Research about creative expression is encouraging. It indicates that engaging in creative activities has significant benefits, such as improved well-being, living longer, being healthier and happier, and having a greater sense of purpose in life.

8. Focus on things that nourish you mentally, physically, spiritually.
   - Find meaningful ways to keep yourself mentally challenged, physically active, and spiritually renewed.

- Mental nourishment — try such things as: puzzles (crosswords, picture puzzles, Sudoku), read, do research on a topic, do genealogy, play cards, enjoy a hobby, take classes.
- Physical exercise — try such things as: going on a walk, hiking, going to the gym. doing water aerobics, trying chair exercises, working in the garden, mowing the lawn, washing the car, going dancing, cleaning the house, cycling.
- Spiritual nourishment — do such things as: meditation, prayer, reading spiritually focused material, dialoguing with others on spiritual topics, going on a retreat alone or with a group for spiritual introspection, volunteering, spending time in nature.
- You feel encouraged when your mind, body and soul are fit and refreshed.

9. Dream big, set goals, and persevere.
   - Dream small, dream medium, dream big. Just dream.
   - Instead of saying, "If only," or "I wish," say, "I can do it," or "I'm going to do it."
   - Remember, it's never too late and you're never too old to do something new and different.
   - It's estimated that 98% of people die without fulfilling their dreams. Do your best to not be one of them.
   - Write your dreams down. There's nothing more encouraging than being able to cross off a dream that you have accomplished.
   - According to some of the research, people with written goals are 50% more likely to achieve them than people without written goals. The act of writing down your goal serves as a powerful motivator.
   - One study suggests that 83% of the U.S. population do not have goals. Let me encourage you to be in the minority.
   - Keep your list up-to-date and adjust it as is appropriate. Cross each one off as you achieve it and then go celebrate. Be proud of yourself. Eliminate those that are no longer ones you want to achieve. Add new ones as you keep dreaming.
   - Never give up.

Before you go, I would like to share a few thoughts about the word, "goodbye." Few people realize that the dictionary meaning of goodbye is "God be with you."

The first recorded use of the word "goodbye" was in 1573. An English writer, Gabriel Harvey, wrote a letter that used the word "Godbwye" in it. "Godbwye" is a contraction of the statement, "God be with ye." Over the years, the word "good" was substituted for "God." Apparently this substitution was influenced by commonly used phrases such as "good day" or "good evening."

In 1882, Jeremiah Rankin composed the hymn, "God Be With You Till We Meet Again." He wanted something to sing when his church choir parted each week. He explained that he wrote it as a Christian goodbye. He got the idea for the song when he became aware that the dictionary definition of "goodbye" was short for "God be with you."

I'm glad we've had the opportunity to say "hello" and share a few words of encouragement. In parting, rather than use the word "goodbye," I think it's much more meaningful and fitting to say, "God be with ye till we meet again." It keeps the door open.

REFLECTION

1. Hello" begins a dialogue and "goodbye" brings it to a close. And "in between" is where memories are made that touch the heart and last a lifetime.
2. May the dreams you hold dearest be those which come true, and the kindness you spread keep returning to you.
3. *May the Lord keep watch between you and me when we are away from each other.* (Genesis 31:49) *And may ....The Lord bless you and keep you; the Lord make his face shine upon you, and be gracious to you; the Lord turn his face toward you, and give you peace."* (Numbers 6:24-26)

SOURCES

The author acknowledges the following references
used in preparation of this text.

BIBICAL QUOTATIONS

All biblical quotations in this book are taken from The Holy Bible, New International Version, Copyright ©1978 by New York International Bible Society. Published by the Zondervan Corporation, Grand Rapids, Michigan, 49506

A CREATIVE SPIRIT DWELLS WITHIN YOU

Cohen, G. (2001). *The Creative Age: Awakening Human Potential in the Second Half of Life.* William Morrow - Harper Collins Publishers, 195 Broadway, New York, NY 10007.

CHOOSE AN "I CAN DO IT" ATTITUDE

Watty, P. (2001). *The Little Engine That Could.* Grosset & Dunlap, 345 Hudson Street 10th Floor, New York, NY 10014.

EMBRACING LIFE'S CHALLENGES

McLeod, S. (May 3, 2008). Erik Erikson's Stages of Psychosocial Development. *Simply Psychology.* Retrieved January 20, 2020, from http://www.simplypsychology.org/ErikErikson.html.

Wikipedia. (2020). *Margaret Brown. Wikipedia.org.* Retrieved January 15, 2020, from wiki/Margaret Brown.

HAVE THE COURAGE TO TURN THE PAGE

Wikipedia. (2020). *Ezra Meeker.* In Wikipedia.org. Retrieved October 5, 2019, from wiki/Ezra Meeker.

GIVE YOURSELF PERMISSION TO BLOOM
Wikipedia. (2020). *Grandma Moses.* In Wikipedia.org. Retrieved October 8, 2019, from wiki/Grandma Moses.

THE AMAZING POWER OF KINDNESS
Wikipedia. (2020). *Random Act of Kindness.* In Wikipedia.org. Retrieved October 15, 2019, from wiki/Random Acts of Kindness.

WHAT DOES IT MEAN TO SAY, "HAVE A NICE DAY"?
Wikipedia. (2020). *Have a Nice Day.* In Wikipedia.org. Retrieved October 16, 2020, from wiki/Have a Nice Day.

THE TALE OF A GRATEFUL WHALE
Fimrite. P. (December 14, 2005). *Daring Rescue of Whale Off Farallones.* SFGATE. Retrieved October 10, 2019, from http://www.sfgate.com.
Gayu. (January 2, 2008). *True Story of a Grateful Whale.* Stories of Kindness from Around the World. Retrieved October 10, 2019, from http://www.kindspring.org.

YOUR LIFE CAN BE MENDED
Wikipedia. (2020) Kintsugi. Wikipedia.org. Retrieved January7, 2020, from wiki/Kintugi.

ACCOMPLISH YOUR GOALS A FEW MINUTES AT A TIMES
Butt, Jr. H. (2005). *Seize the Moment.* The High Calling: Theology of Work Project. Retrieved *October10, 2019, from* http://dev.theologyofwork.org.

THE FIVE-FOLD PHILOSOPHY OF THE ANT
Wikipedia. (2020). *Wright Brothers.* Wikipedia.org. Retrieved September 20, 2019, from wiki/Wright Brothers.

MAY YOU BE BLESSED WITH AN ANAM CARA (SOUL-MATE)
Wikipedia. (2019). *Anam Cara.* Wikipedia.org. Retrieved August 14, 2019, from wiki/Anam Cara.

A HUG IS WORTH MORE THAN A THOUSAND WORDS

Nguyen, T. (December 6, 2017). *Hacking Into Your Happy Chemicals: Dopamine, Serotonin, Endorphins and Oxytocin*. Huff Post. Retrieved October 10, 2019 from www.huffpost.com.

Hasin,D., Pampori, Z., Aarif, O., Bulbul, K., Sheikh, A., & Bhat, I. (2018). *"Happy hormones and their significance in animals and man."* International Journal of Veterinary Sciences and Animal Husbandry, 3 (5), pp. 100-103.

HOW A PIGEON CHANGED MY PERSPECTIVE

Wikipedia. (2020). Cher Ami. Wikipedia.org. *Retrieved October 11, 2019, from http://wikipedia.org.*

Bieniek, A. (n.d.). Cher Ami: The Pigeon that Saved the Lost Battalion. Retrieved October 11, 2019 from http://www.worldwar1centennial.org.

GET A BUCKET AND MAKE A LIST

Periyakoil, V. (February 8,2018). "Talk to Your Doctor About Your Bucket List." The New York Times. Accessed October16, 2019.

IT'S NEVER TOO LATE TO DREAM

Wikipedia. (2020). *Ray Kroc*. Wikipedia.org. Retrieved February 10, 2020 from wiki/Ray Kroc.

QUALITIES OF INDIVIDUALS WHO ACHIEVE THEIR GOALS

Chen, R. (April, 2012). *30 Qualities That Make Ordinary People Extraordinary*. Retrieved October 15, 2019, from http://www.embracepossibility.com.

Wikipedia. (2020). *Bethany Hamilton*. Wikipedia.org. Retrieved February 11, 2020 from wiki/Bethany Hamilton.

Wikipedia. (2020). *Henry Ford*. Wikipedia.org. Retrieved February 11, 2020 from wiki/Henry Ford.

Wikipedia. (2020). *Benjamin Franklin*. Wikipedia.org. Retrieved February 11, 2020 from wiki/Benjamin Franklin.

MAKE SOMETHING GOOD HAPPEN
BETWEEN "HELLO" AND "GOODBYE"

Wikipedia. (2020). *Skype*. Wikipedia.org. Retrieved October 11. 2019, from wiki/Skype.

APPENDIX A

WHO DO YOU SEE IN THE MANGER?

Shepherd boy, O shepherd boy,
Who do you see in the manger?
Do you see the son of God?
Do you see your creator?
Do you see God's gift to you?
Do you see your Savior?

He is the Prince of Peace.
The mighty God is he.
He has come to deliver us.
He has come to set us free.
Hallelujah, hallelujah.
He has come to set us free.

Shepherd boy, O Shepherd boy,
Who do you see in the manger?
Do you see the mother Mary,
In her arms her baby boy?
Do you hear the angel's singing?
Do you hear their song of joy?

He is the Prince of Peace.
The mighty God is he.
He has come to deliver us.
He has come to set us free.

Hallelujah, hallelujah.
He has come to set us free.

Shepherd boy, O shepherd boy,
Who do you see in the manger?
Do you see God's gift of love?
Do you see the Holy One?
Do you see the Lord of Glory,
God's only begotten son?

He is the Prince of Peace.
The mighty God is he.
He has come to deliver us.
He has come to set us free.
Oh Hallelujah, hallelujah.
He has come to set us free.

by Dr. Charles Milton Lee

APPENDIX B

AN IRISH BLESSING FOR CHILDREN

May the good Lord bless and keep you,
May angels guide your way;
May you always walk in sunshine,
With a rainbow in each day.

May the sounds of laughter bless you,
May faithful friends be yours;
May your heart be filled with kindness,
And a love that long endures.

May your days be filled with blessings,
Like the sun lights up the sky;
And like the birds that soar above you,
May you spread your wings and fly

May your life be filled with dreaming,
And may all your dreams come true;
And where ere you choose to go in life,
May the Lord watch over you.

—by Dr. Charles Milton Lee

ACKNOWLEDGEMENTS

- My wife, Muriel, whose consistent support and patience encouraged me and helped keep me motivated.
- My family, Luanne/John, Claudia/John, Denver/Kathy, Darren/Kim for their support, suggestions and encouragement.
- Danny Shuler, my friend and fellow coffee partner, who served as my accountability partner and offered encouraging, spiritual dialogue.
- Nikki Johnson, my sister-in-law, who read the manuscript several times, gave suggestions, and offered encouragement.
- David Moore, my former classmate and friend, who read the manuscript and offered valuable feedback.
- Chandler Bolt and the Self-Publishing School for guiding me through the whole process of publishing a book.
- Matt Stone and the staff at 100 Covers for their creative cover design, as well as Jason and the rest of the staff at Formatted Books.

Do You Like to Write?

Would You Like to Publish a Book?

Discover

SELF-PUBLISHING SCHOOL'S

3-Step Blueprint

you need to become a bestselling author in as little as

3 MONTHS.

Even if you're busy, bad at writing, or don't know where to start, you CAN write a bestseller and build your best life.

They helped me and they will help you.

Visit·

https://self-publishingschool.com/friend/

They'll get you to the finish line.

SHARE YOUR THOUGHTS

Every author appreciates honest feedback.
Feedback helps a writer improve....and I want to improve.

If you would like to **WRITE A REVIEW** of this book,
it's an easy process. Please follow the steps below.

1. **Go to Amazon.com and sign in.** You must be an Amazon customer to leave a review and you must have made a $50 purchase or more.

2. **Go to the book,** *ENCOURAGEMENT For Such a Time as This.*

3. Under the heading **Customer Reviews,** you will see a button for **write a customer review.** Click on it and you will be taken to a page set up for 'Your Review."

4. **Select the rating** of the book from 1-5 stars, with 5 being the best score.

5. **Write your review** in the box. Keep in mind if you leave this page before submitting you will have to start over. (You might want to write the review first in Word or Evernote and then copy and paste.)

6. **Create a headline** for your review.

7. **Hit submit.** Your review will go live within a couple of hours, although it can take up to 24 hours or more.

THANK YOU.